# CONTENTS

...ish politics

the first year of the scot...ish

parliament and beyond

edited by gerry hassan and
chris warhurst

foreword by gordon brewer

*BT Scotland*
*Bringing all Scotland together*

The
Stationery
Office

© The Stationery Office 2000

A CIP catalogue record for this book is available from the British Library
A Library of Congress CIP catalogue record has been applied for

First published 2000

ISBN 0 11 497280 X

## Section Four: Civic Scotland, Identities and the Isles

# LIST OF TABLES

the new scottish politics **the first year of the scottish parliament and beyond**

# CONTRIBUTORS

Rowena Arshad is Director of the Centre for Education for Racial Equality in Scotland (CERES)

David Bell is Professor of Economics at the University of Stirling

Gordon Brewer is presenter of BBC *Newsnight Scotland*

Alice Brown is Professor of Politics at the University of Edinburgh and co-founder of the Governance of Scotland Forum

Laura Brown is a pupil of class 10 at Richmond Park School, Glasgow

Noreen Burrows is John Monnet Professor of European Law at the University of Glasgow

John Curtice is Professor of Government at the University of Strathclyde and Deputy Director of the Centre for Research into Elections and Social Trends (CREST)

Fraser Doherty is a pupil of Class 7B at Davidson's Main Primary School, Edinburgh

Sheila Dow is Professor in Economics at the University of Stirling

David T. Evans is Senior Lecturer in Sociology at the University of Glasgow

Robina Goodlad is Professor of Housing and Urban Studies at the University of Glasgow

Gerry Hassan is Head of Communications at the Scottish Council for Development and Industry (SCDI)

Robert Hazell is Director of the Constitution Unit at the School of Public Policy, University College London

Peter Jones is Scotland and North of England Correspondent of *The Economist*

Richard Kerley is Director of the MBA Programme at the University of Edinburgh Management School

Elinor Kelly is Honourary Research Fellow in Race and Ethnic Issues at the University of Glasgow

Janice Kirkpatrick is Director of the design company Graven Images

Peter Lynch is Lecturer in Politics at the University of Stirling

Angela McCabe is a Politics student at Manchester Metropolitan University

James McCormick is Research Director of the Scottish Council Foundation

Jean McFadden is Lecturer in Public Law at the University of Strathclyde

Catherine Macleod is Political Editor of The *Herald*

Lynne MacMillan is a consultant with GPC Scotland and formerly Head of Legal Policy at the Scottish Consumer Council

Lucy McTernan is Assistant Director of Scottish Council for Voluntary Organisations (SCVO)

Iain Macwhirter is a political commentator, presenter of BBC's *Holyrood* programme and a regular columnist in The *Herald* and *Sunday Herald*

Colin Mair is Director of the Scottish Local Authorities Management Centre at the University of Strathclyde

James Mitchell is Professor of Politics at the University of Sheffield

Richard Parry is Lecturer in Social Policy at the University of Edinburgh

Lindsay Paterson is Professor of Educational Policy at the University of Edinburgh and editor of *Scottish Affairs*

Harry Perdikou is a pupil of Class P7A at Davidson's Main Primary School, Edinburgh

Robert Pyper is Director of the Centre for Public Policy and Management at Glasgow Caledonian University

Douglas Robertson is Director of the Housing Policy and Practice Unit at the University of Stirling and Chair of Partick Housing Association, Glasgow

Philip Schlesinger is Director of the Media Research Institute at the University of Stirling

TAG Theatre Company is Scotland's national theatre company for young people

Chris Warhurst is Senior Lecturer in Human Resource Management at the University of Strathclyde

Allan Watt is Director of Development at the WISE Group

Tracey White is Assistant Secretary of the Scottish Trades Union Congress (STUC)

Andy Wightman is a writer specialising in land reform

Robin Wilson is Director of Democratic Dialogue

# ACKNOWLEDGEMENTS

The first year of the Scottish Parliament has been a steep learning curve for many within and outwith the Parliament. The production of this book has in many ways mirrored that experience. We have tried to be ambitious - bringing together the best academics, writers and commentators in their fields from within and outwith Scotland to analyse the first year, assess whether things lived up to expectations and to have a look at future trends.

The changing pace of events and unforseen developments made the production of this book a sometimes nerve racking one both for ourselves and the contributors. More than once during the course of the editing, authors have had to rewrite sections on the basis of new and expected events. Our biggest thanks go to all of the contributors to this book who bore impossible headlines and requests with good humour and patience. We hope that they think the same of us.

This book is different from our previous publications in that it has very different types of contributions - with alongside the conventional chapters, short pieces from young people from the TAG Theatre Congress of Nations project and reflections on some of the most noteworthy events of the last year. It has not been our intention to include a comprehensive guide to every event in the last year, and readers who wish to read in say, education and health are advised to look at our *A Different Future: A Modernisers' Guide to Scotland* which came out last year.

We and our contributors have been aided in the production of this book by a host of people too numerous to mention in full. However, in particular, we would like to thank Johanna Reilly of The Stationery Office, Edinburgh and the sponsorship of BT Scotland and support of Brendan Dick and Tony Spence. Jon Morgan, Director of TAG Theatre, was also extremely supportive and successfully conveyed the enthusiasm and imagination of the Congress of Nations project.

Elaine Blaxter of the University of Strathclyde provided superb librarian support, and Suzanne Young of the same university secretarial support. Lastly, for their perseverance with their partners, we would like to thank Rosie Ilett and Lee Murray. Rosie, a qualified librarian, amongst her many talents, also gave her time and expertise in compiling the index.

We hope that you enjoy the book as much as we did putting it together. It is an historic document: an examination of the work in progress that is the building of Scotland's fledgling democracy. It has been written as a positive contribution to that, and we hope people will read it in the spirit of optimism with which we put it together.

Gerry Hassan                                    Chris Warhurst

June 2000

# FOREWORD

**Gordon Brewer**

A few months before Holyrood officially opened the door on the new Scotland, I was asked by BBC2 to make a documentary about how the country was changing. My abiding memory is not of any grand politician's words, but of a folk musician whose band entered the *Herald*'s 'Song for Scotland' competition. After an interview, he apologised for having little to say. He felt so disenfranchised, he said, that he had not thought seriously about politics for years.

It is worth bearing that in mind as we try to orient ourselves amidst the cacophony that is Scottish politics in the new millennium. No matter how absurd some of the posturing, no matter how distasteful some of the noise - and some of the contributors to this volume positively hate what they are hearing - the most important fact is there is noise where there was silence. One way of interpreting recent poll results is that while people in Scotland show scant respect for their politicians, they want them in a forum where they can be disrespected properly.

It would be difficult now for even the most apathetic resident of Scotland not to think about politics. Things have changed and changed utterly, if often unexpectedly. For example, while everyone expected the Parliament would make a difference, all of us, I suspect from the First Minister downwards, failed to anticipate what a difference a Scottish government would make. Politics in the new Scotland is largely, as in London, driven by events, not model parliamentary debates. Suddenly everything from Orcadian fields sown with GM-tainted rape seed to last winter's 'flu epidemic is, and is seen to be, the responsibility of Edinburgh.

With that shift in real power has come a huge shift in perception. Even those newspapers which most denigrate Holyrood and all its ways now spend much of their time reporting it. And even those who agree with Cardinal Thomas Winning that the Parliament has been an 'utter failure' would have to concede it is a failure which now occupies much of the political space. They may be disgusted, but they are certainly no longer disenfranchised.

Sometimes the extent of the change, not so much in institutions as in the political and intellectual climate which has accompanied those institutions, can best be glimpsed through absences. Absences which are so absent they are in danger of being forgotten. In the spring of this year I worked on a short film for *Newsnight* in London about the Parliament's first year. An editor in London insisted that I reflect 'the debate over the Parliament'. I thought he meant tuition fees or the Freedom of Information Act or the trivial, if entertaining, scandals which have sometimes threatened to blight the past twelve months. 'No, the debate over the Parliament,' he insisted. Eventually I got the point. It is of course perfectly understandable for someone based in London to think that there is a huge debate in Scotland over the merits of devolution and, once one thinks about it, is striking that there is not. Even Cardinal Winning, I suspect, means that Holyrood should follow his moral agenda, not that it should be abolished. Compare and contrast the atmosphere as recently as the last general election campaign.

Also striking is how there has been a subtle, but marked, shift in the topics of rumination. At a recent conference, Wendy Alexander, the Minister for Communities, remarked that there is a lot less navel gazing in Scotland these days and I think she is right. The politics of identity tends to flourish in societies where there is no politics proper, or at least a perception that there is no politics proper. Even the arguments for independence these days seem more straightforwardly political, rather than an excuse for soul searching. This, surely, has to be a good thing. Scotland has done enough rummaging in its past to discover what kind of society it is. Now, hopefully, we can just get on with inventing that society.

It may be the case, as Gerry Hassan and Chris Warhurst argue in their introduction to this book, that there is a need for the new politicians to develop a coherent narrative which explains their purpose, although arguably that is a matter for the political parties, and hence for plurality. But I doubt if there is a need for much more than that. Some of us have had bad experiences with meta-narratives and would sooner leave them in the cupboard and get on with other things.

There has been another aspect to this first year, something which bubbles just under the surface of most of the contributions to this book. If the new Scotland is in the process of invention, it is also in the process of revelation. If I were a government spin doctor then the best face I could put on the Section 28 debate is that at least it has allowed us to see where things stand. But it is not just on combustible issues such as Section 28. Much of John Curtice's contribution to this book is based on data collected at the time of last year's Scottish elections, data which over time should evolve into a Scottish social attitudes survey. That is exciting because at the moment, rather surprisingly, we simply do not know what people living in Scotland think. And, hopefully, this will simply be the beginning - the collection of more data on the Scottish economy, for example, is a matter of some urgency.

But if the revelation has been, well, revealing, the invention has, so far, been hesitant. As Hassan and Warhurst point out, to a large extent in the new Scottish politics 'it is still constitutional and institutional issues which are being played out'. This is partly because, at this stage, almost every detailed policy issue carries a constitutional affect - there is little of the constitution in tuition fees, for example, yet it was the first new area in which the Scottish system varied significantly from the English. Indeed, as the Mike Tyson affair showed, at the moment anything can have constitutional implications. And, to be fair, after a hesitant start during which the new MSPs seemed intent on a collective hunt for banana skins, the Parliament is only now beginning to concern itself with substantial legislation.

Not that the MSPs have been faultless. Iain Macwhirter argues this has been 'a Jekyll and Hyde Parliament', reported by a media which often seems closely acquainted with the latter but oblivious of the former. It is hard to deny that the media portrayal of Holyrood has often seemed to owe more to comic strips than literature.

A truce might involve a recognition of faults on both sides, faults which are almost mirror images. If the Scottish media has, with some notable exceptions, focused on trivia at the expense of policy, then the politicians have, arguably, failed to realise that in politics the colourful and controversial are often more fateful than the seriously intellectual. Leaving aside the merits of the arguments for and against repeal, how many members of the Scottish Executive would, with the benefit of hindsight, want Section 28 to be seen as the defining issue of their first year? No more surely than Bill Clinton really wanted the issue of gays in the military to be the defining moment of his first year. On the other side, it would be sobering to count the number of column inches devoted to, say, Mike Tyson's visit to Scotland with the number devoted to, say, Scotland's role in the new economy.

That said, there remains much inventing to do. Already the Parliament has flexed its muscles in some very unWestminster ways. The debate over warrant sales was almost as important for the procedural issues it raised as the substance of the issue itself. With three parliamentary committees having given the green light to the bill, MSPs queued up to argue that the Scottish Executive simply could not veto it given all the previous brouhaha about the enhanced role of Holyrood committees and how they would compensate for the lack of a second chamber. It was a defining moment, establishing that this Parliament really is different, that it is a legislature prepared to exert its right over its Executive and, not least, that whatever their faults, the Parliament's members are not prepared to play the role of lobby fodder so familiar in Another Place. Listening to the warrant sales debate, it struck me that what I was hearing was more reminiscent of a debate in the US Congress than Westminster.

However, as Robin Wilson discusses in the latter part of this book, the spirit of the new does not stop at the border with England. A country in which 'federalism' has been a dirty word not to be spoken in front of the children is slowly waking to the fact it is now a de facto federation. While we are only beginning to work out the implications of this development, the one rather obvious fact is that civilisation as we know it has not come to an end. Tuition fees are different in Scotland, but the UK education system has not collapsed under the weight of its own contradictions. Scotland will have a differing Freedom of Information Act, but it is far from clear that we will face legalised anarchy.

One thing which is becoming clear is that devolution may throw up as many political as constitutional problems. For example, it is easy enough to argue that differing tuition fees cause few if any institutional problems. It is less easy to justify politically, if you are a Labour Party member, for example, why English students deserve to pay tuition fees upfront while their Scottish colleagues do not. In this sense, devolution may yet provide scope for an interesting provocation to the UK system as a whole.

The chapters in this book are part of a work in progress. Enjoy them. And always bear in mind the subtext of their significance - that in large part they are dealing with subjects which just over a dozen months ago simply did not exist.

# CHAPTER 1: a new politics?

**gerry hassan and
chris warhurst**

The institutions of the British state have been defined by their conservatism and their slow, evolutionary adapting to the times. By British standards then a constitutional revolution has occurred in the last few years which has radically changed and re-engineered the institutions of the British state. Within two years of a Labour government coming to power at a UK level, a Scottish Parliament and Welsh Assembly were established, the process of real devolution to Northern Ireland begun and progress made on reform of regional and city representative assemblies in England. Moreover, devolution has taken on a life of its own. In Scotland, the Cubie Committee recommendations distinguished student funding from that of England and Wales - much to the consternation of the Department for Education and Employment; in Wales, Rhodri Morgan is now established as First Secretary, while in the London mayoral elections, Ken Livingstone stood and won as an independent - both despite the blocking attempts of Downing Street.

The Scottish Parliament and Executive are little over one year old and in that period they have begun to get to grips with the challenges and opportunities of governing Scotland. There have been - as there are bound to be in any process of building new institutions - many mistakes, crises and resignations (see Table 1 below). However, there have also been significant policy advances across a range of areas from the Incapable Adults Bill, to tuition fees and warrant sales. And it has been a period of immense change at the level of UK institutions with implications for how the Scottish Parliament relates to Westminster, Cardiff and Belfast (see Table 2). Thus, we need to get a sense of proportion when we examine the record of the Scottish Parliament and Executive, and acknowledge that this is 'unfinished business' - both at a Scottish and UK level.

# A YEAR OF CULTURAL SCHIZOPHRENIA

The first year can be seen, as Iain Macwhirter describes in Chapter Two, as one of 'cultural schizophrenia' - of the Parliament and Scotland's institutions slowly developing new roles and voices, while, cynicism and self-doubt is whipped up by the press and others. Macwhirter calls this 'the Jekyll and Hyde Parliament' - of growing self-confidence on one level, and self-hatred and putting down on the other. The concern is the character of the Parliament that is emerging, with some commentators being more dismissive than others, as Tom Nairn (2000: 262) indicated recently when he suggested that:

> *No one really thinks the shade of William Wallace will reappear at Holyrood. A lot of people do think, with appropriate despondency, that Councillor McDirge, Provost McBaffie and Mrs. McGrunge will not only be in there but could soon swamp the place.*

Such comments reflect a wider re-awakening of debate and discussion about the character of Scotland itself, and how that character can be shaped by the Parliament and those who sit in it as MSPs. This debate and discussion has been made most stark in the furore over Section 28/Clause 2A. Asked in the 1999 Scottish Election Survey whether homosexual relations are always wrong, 24 per cent of Scottish (and 25 per cent of English) respondents agreed affirmatively, down six per cent from the 30 per cent of Scots agreeing with this statement in 1992. Asked whether we should be more tolerant of unconventional lives, 59 per cent of Scottish (and 47 per cent of English) respondents agreed (Brown et al, forthcoming 2001). These findings show unambiguously that Scotland is at least as tolerant, if not on some measures, more tolerant than England, and is becoming increasingly so. What is also evident from the survey findings is that a vociferous minority of Scots are more intolerant of others rights, but that this is not the equality lobby, but the moral authoritarians associated with the Keep the Clause campaign. Nevertheless, the Scottish political classes across all parties seem ill-equipped to argue a positive and coherent case for equality in the face of the Keep the Clause campaign. Instead, the Scrap the Clause lobby became increasing defensive, even self-loathing:

> *Make way for the Lumpen Scot. Habitat: largely the West of Scotland but found in large numbers across the country. Predominantly, but not exclusively male, traits are: aggressive, pig*

*ignorant, loud, sexist. Health: one in two will contract cancer of some form, and his testicles are a carcinogenic war zone. Lifestyle: inert. Culture: football, football and football. Prospects: redundancy. Age: immaterial. Fears: profound sense of sexual and social insecurity - hates gays and English.*

(Macwhirter, 2000a: 4)

If it is, as Elaine C. Smith claims, about 'redneck' Scotland (Sinclair, 2000) rather than Red Clydeside, then it is about contested meanings of Scotland. To some advocates on both sides this is a fight for the very soul and moral fibre of Scotland and in its symbolism and significance, the Section 28/Clause 2A debate has many similarities with the debate over James MacMillan's 'Scotland's Shame' lecture on the degree of anti-Catholic prejudice in Scotland (MacMillan, 2000).

Certainly the business as usual 'cheque book' politics of Brian Souter brings into question the 'new politics' hoped for by the Scottish Constitutional Convention and analysed by Alice Brown in Chapter Six. And it is ironic that the most prominent event to occur in its first year was a referendum that sought to by-pass the long-fought for and newly established Scottish Parliament. Herein lies a key feature of the first year of the Parliament: it is still constitutional and institutional issues which are being played out. In addition to the Souter referendum, media and public attention has focused on the 'turf war' between the First Minister and the Secretary of State for Scotland, MSPs salaries, the issue of special advisers, 'Lobbygate', the cost of the new parliamentary building and the medallions given to MSPs. Perhaps part of the problem lies in the commonly held belief that the Parliament would usher in a new wave of politicians who could and would immediately articulate a pre-prepared vision of the new Scotland.

## ANATOMY OF THE NEW SCOTLAND

Scotland's 129 new MSPs have been subject to a mass of criticism and scorn since they were first elected. Some of this attention is just over-enthusiastic scrutiny of a large press pool dieting on just two days each week of visually and reportably exciting parliamentary activity on the Main Chamber floor. However, some of it simply resonated with the Scottish tradition of self-doubt, with the degree of insult flung at Labour women MSPs - 'the shoal of Karens' debate - spectacularly missing the point.

A common hope prior to the 1999 elections was that MSPs would be very different from their Westminster Scots MPs. MSPs would be less likely to be party hacks, there would be more independents or independently minded MSPs, they would come from a broad spectrum of life, with more women, less councillors and be substantially younger.

This popular belief that MSPs are different is still remarkably strong, despite evidence to the contrary. Apart from the remarkable breakthrough in terms of women - 49 MSPs versus 12 MPs sitting for Scottish constituencies - placing Scotland third in the international table of gender equality versus Westminster's placing at 26th - MSPs and MPs are remarkable similar and drawn from similar parts of society (1). There is a preponderance of public sector backgrounds - whether it be local government, universities or public services, but a more sizeable grouping from the private sector and business world than Westminster. There is a similar number of ex-councillors in Holyrood and Westminster - 51 at Holyrood (40 per cent) and 33 at Westminster (46 per cent). The Labour groups in each have similar numbers of ex-councillors: 23 out of 56 at Holyrood and 30 out of 56 at Westminster. The Liberal Democrats have the highest portion of ex-councillors - 10 out of 17 MSPs. One difference which is pronounced is the number of ex-council leaders at Holyrood: 15, of whom 10 sit on Labour benches (while another one, Independent Dennis Canavan sat as a Labour council leader).

Similarly, despite popular belief, MSPs are not substantially younger than MPs. The average age of MSPs when elected was 45 years, while of Scots MPs it was 49. There is very little difference between the parties with Labour MSPs being an average 43 years and SNP MSPs 45 years, while Labour Westminster MPs are on average 49 years. It is true that there are seven MSPs in their twenties at Holyrood compared to one at Westminster and more in their thirties in Holyrood than Westminster (a ratio of 30:6), but this comparative youth is counterbalanced by the number of older MSPs. One factor which has also contributed towards a perception of MSPs as younger has been the presence of a significant number of thirtysomethings in the Scottish Executive - the McConnells, Alexanders and Deacons - and a spread of twenty and thirtysomethings in the SNP leadership.

Another perception is that MSPs are generally more educated than their Westminster counterparts. Only 12 MSPs never attended university or a further or higher education institute, compared to 10 MPs; this difference is slightly more pronounced with Labour with 6 out of its 56 MSPs and 10 out of 56 MPs having no further or higher education. However, it can be said that in this area, MSPs and MPs have mirrored the changing nature of Scottish society where participation in further and higher education has become the expectation rather than the exception.

## POPULAR EXPECTATIONS OF THE PARLIAMENT

Before May 6th 1999, the Scottish people had high expectations for their Parliament. Both the 1997 Scottish Election and Referendum Surveys recorded that across a range of economic and social issues - devolved and reserved - Scots believed that the Parliament would make a difference. The latter survey showed that while 76 per cent expected taxes to go up, 70 per cent expected improvements in education, 65 per cent in the NHS and 64 per cent in the economy (Brown et al., 1999: 118; Surridge and McCrone, 1999: 46; Denver et al, 2000: 200).

The scale of these expectations was never going to be met, particularly early on when the Parliament and its politicians were finding their feet. However a number of points need to be disentangled. Support for the Parliament remains strong and is likely to continue. An *Economist* survey showed Scots thought the most powerful institution in 20 years would be the Scottish Parliament with 46 per cent, the European Union 31 per cent and Westminster 8 per cent (The *Economist*, 1999). However, there is some disillusionment with the Parliament. A BBC Survey on May 9th 2000 indicated that most respondents (43 per cent) were indifferent to the Parliament, although of those expressing an opinion, most were unhappy with it. Nevertheless, the same survey showed that a clear majority of 60 per cent wished that the Parliament had more powers, a demand even amongst those critical of its performance. We would suggest that this dissonance arises because the public can distinguish between the promise of the Parliament on the one hand, and the current behaviour of its politicians and the media reporting of that behaviour on the other.

As we mentioned earlier, too much emphasis remains on constitutional and institutional issues when Scots want policy changes that will improve their lives. At the moment, the Parliament has begun in its first year to slowly shift into 'delivery mode' on policy as described by Peter Jones in Chapter Seven and Lynne MacMillan in Chapter Twelve, but the media has not wanted to report this, preferring tales of scandals and crises. This perhaps reflects a wider point about the Parliament's legislative priorities not yet capturing the popular imagination. Real and substantive policy initiatives have emerged, on warrant sales, freedom of information, land reform, student tuition fees, housing and health. These have involved complex stories which the media often covered in terms of personality politics but which involved real change and sometimes had wider implications for UK policy.

## THE CHANGING FACE OF POLITICS: FUTURE SCENARIOS

The Scottish political system - long defined and distorted by Labour's one party dominance which shaped an asymmetrical system of party competition - is slowly shifting to a more pluralist, fragmented political system. Several different scenarios are possible here:

- Labour continues its historic role as Scotland's leading party on a slightly lower vote and with a more competitive political system.

- Labour and SNP develop a two party system with the Liberal Democrats and Conservatives reduced to marginal players - this scenario looked likely in the summer of 1998 when the SNP built up a significant lead in the polls over Labour with the Lib Dems and Tories reduced to single figures.

- A hyper-pluralist politics, whereby Labour and the SNP's vote is reduced by intense competition not only from the Lib Dems and Tories, but 'new' forces such as the Scottish Socialist Party (SSP) and Scottish Greens.

This last scenario would not be a proper six party system but would, link into electoral trends across the Western world, which herald the end of neat, two party politics and one-party dominance. Instead, it would offer two major, two minor and two micro parties - an alignment that is currently a possibility in the polls given the relative success of the SSP and Greens. At the Hamilton South and Ayr by-elections, the SSP scored respectively an impressive 9 per cent and 4 per cent - taking disillusioned Labour voters that the SNP was desperately trying to win. Already the SSP has a more significant level of electoral support in Parliamentary by-elections than Jim Sillars much talked about Scottish Labour Party managed in the 1970s.

The present balance of electoral forces also suggests that a non-Labour majority will at some point come to power and that this will coalesce around the SNP. This point - perhaps not at the next Scottish Parliament elections, but the one after that - will be a defining point for Scottish politics. It will bring the principle of alternating in power into the centre of Scottish politics and with it such concepts as alternative governments and 'swing' parties which decide who can put together a parliamentary majority. Labour will need to develop a less institutionalised form of politics and become more conversant with the politics of pluralism and partnership at national and local level. The SNP will have to transform itself from an opportunist catch-all party embracing simultaneously traditional social democracy and Thatcherism - to becoming a party with a defined core set of beliefs beyond independence. And both parties, if Scotland is to avoid damaging start-stop-start policy missives from rotating governments, will need to develop a consensus about the character of a new Scotland to be pursued.

## DISPLACING MYTHS, FUTURE VISIONS

In the last year, a number of narratives about Scotland have been challenged. The myth of civic Scotland that it is a land with rich, complex, progressive institutions and opinion just waiting to contribute to 'the new politics' has been severely undermined. This myth suggested that if the political processes could be fine-tuned to get the right consultative processes then civic Scotland would provide the appropriate input to arrive at the correct policy output. This was always a romantic delusion, but the debate over Section 28/Clause 2A has shown that Scottish civil society is just as full of contradictions as elsewhere and has powerful forces of narrow, backward looking conservatism.

Another pivotal myth was that of labourist Scotland, which asserted that Scottish Labour won elections in the 1980s, while English Labour lost them because the former was radical and connected to the people. This theory reached its absurd levels by seeing new Labour as an English creation, irrelevant to the needs of Scotland. Scottish Labour's lack of sureness not just in the first year of the Parliament, but since Labour was elected in 1997 at a UK level has shown the lack of a radical vision and ideas in the party.

The other central myth was that of nationalist Scotland which exaggerated the degree of difference between Scotland and England to aid the argument for independence or greater autonomy. This postulated that Scotland was a social democratic country which had held out against Thatcherism, whereas England had abandoned any sense of care, compassion and centre-left values. This simplistic dichotomy allowed the Scots to feel morally superior to the English. One year of devolution has already shown that Scots people want Scottish solutions to Scottish problems, but that most people share the same values and policies as English people: a broadly social democratic, centre-left agenda.

What this has meant is that the last myth of Scotland has been shown to be grounded in reality - of Scotland as a social democratic country - defined as support for egalitarian values, social justice, redistribution, regulation of the market for the common good, support for collective as well as individual interests, and advancement of democratic citizenship and active government (see Giddens, 1998; Sassoon, 1999). The direction of several of the key policy debates in the last year - on Cubie, Section 28, economic policy, social inclusion and quangos - shows the social democratic consensus that exists in Scotland. What is surprising, given the extent to which this discourse had become identified with an oppositionalist politics during the Tory years, is how quickly it has moved onto an agenda of positive, innovative policy.

One of the problems in the first year has been the lack of a convincing narrative from the political classes about what the process of devolution is meant to be about. In practice, devolution has brought about a host of policy changes, but 'the bigger picture' of which these policies are part is sadly missing. It would be a shame if the bigger picture that was allowed to emerge was one reduced to a 'politics of region' (Macwhirter, 2000b) with the nations, regions and cities of the UK engaged in a zero-sum game vying with each other for larger slices of the restricted public funding cake. Instead the bigger picture should locate devolution in the shift from an oppositional social democracy - as characterised Scottish politics in the 1980s - to an aspirational, achieving social democracy.

For this wider story to be told, we will need a greater sense of imagination and self-confidence from our political classes and leadership across society, reclaiming the relevance of politics and reconnecting to different visions of the future and progress (Hassan and Warhurst, 1999). If devolution is to succeed as a process which is about real and substantial change, rather than just institutional autonomy, then new political leadership will need to find their voices on 'the bigger picture' - telling the story of a different Scotland with a different future. This will involve confronting difficult truths about the character of Scotland, challenging vested interests and elites and developing policies which address the structural inequalities which disfigure Scottish society and lives (see Mooney and Johnstone, 2000).

To be effective, this narrative will have to resonate with the lived experience of Scots. The political leadership, therefore, will need to be grounded in their analysis of the current and possible character of Scotland. Evidence based policy is thus a requisite. For too long, as David Blunkett (2000) recently admitted, government and the civil service have been a 'knowledge free zone'. Care must be made, however, to avoid a contrived approach to evidence based policy in which the Executive or a parliamentary committee would decide a policy and then seek evidence to support it, discarding anything contradictory. Better practice would be for an issue to be identified, evidence gathered and considered, and then policy determined (see Wilson, 2000 on the experience of Northern Ireland). This approach requires new inputs to and processes in policy-making. For example, there needs to be a wider enfranchisement of individuals and groups engaging in policy-making: the emerging 'clientism' identified by Peter Lynch in Chapter Eight has to be vigorously challenged. The civil service also needs to be more outward looking, aided by inward and outward secondments, and change from being the guardians of conservatism to the champions of modernisation.

Aside from debates about the term 'modernisation' as it relates to the reconfiguring of the Labour Party, Scotland needs modernisation; with better health, housing, jobs and education. The public have a sense that the Parliament can bring about change for the better in Scotland and know that large swathes of society are crying out for fundamental change, yet they also feel alienated from politics and politicians. The challenge to the Scottish Parliament and 'the new politics' in this environment is immense, but much progress has been made in the first twelve months. Whether the Parliament can live up to expectations is another matter, but the first year has seen the first, hesitant, nervous, steps towards the new Scotland. There are still many more to be taken.

## Table 1: The First Year of the Scottish Parliament

**1999:**

| | |
|---|---|
| May 6 | First Scottish Parliament Elections |
| May 12 | David Steel elected Presiding Officer |
| May 13 | Donald Dewar elected First Minister with 71 votes to Alex Salmond's 35, David McLetchie's 18, Dennis Canavan 3 |

| | |
|---|---|
| May 14 | Labour-Lib Dem Partnership for Scotland signed |
| May 17 | Labour-Lib Dem Executive announced of 11 ministers; John Reid succeeds Donald Dewar as Secretary of State |
| May 18 | 11 junior ministers announced |
| May 30 | Pat Robertson, US evangelical preacher involved in a deal with the Bank of Scotland, denounces Scotland as a 'dark land' dominated by homosexuals |
| June 5 | Bank of Scotland pulls out of deal with Pat Robertson |
| June 16 | Donald Dewar presents the Government's first legislative programme containing a total of eight bills |
| June 17 | Parliament approves Holyrood Building by 66-57 votes |
| July 1 | Scottish Parliament officially opened by HRH Queen Elizabeth II |
| July 2 | Parliament sets up Independent Committee on Tuition Fees by 70-48 votes |
| July 5-August 30 | First Parliamentary Summer Recess |
| Aug. 9 | James MacMillan delivers his 'Scotland's Shame' lecture on anti-Catholic prejudice |
| Aug. 31 | Mental Health (Public Safety and Appeals) (Scotland) Bill introduced |
| Sept. 13 | Mental Health Act receives Royal Assent |
| Sept. 23 | Labour win Westminster seat of Hamilton South with majority cut from 15,878 to 556 over the SNP |
| Sept. 26 | 'Lobbygate' publication in The Observer about Beattie Media, Kevin Reid, John Reid's son and Jack McConnell |
| Oct. 29 | Wendy Alexander, Minister for Communities announces abolition of Section 28 |

| Dec. 1 | Public Finance and Accountability (Scotland) Bill passes all parliamentary stages |
| Dec. 9 | John Rafferty, Donald Dewar's Special Adviser resigns |
| Dec. 21 | Cubie Committee Report on Tuition Fees published |

**2000:**

| Jan. 17 | Public Finance and Accountability (Scotland) Act receives Royal Assent |
| Jan. 25 | Philip Chalmers, Head of the Strategic Communications Unit resigns |
| Jan. 27 | Scottish Executive proposals on abolishing tuition fees agreed by 68-53 votes |
| Feb. 10 | Budget (Scotland) Bill passes all parliamentary stages, Scottish Parliament votes 88-17 against a Conservative motion supporting retention of Section 28 |
| Feb. 17 | Lord Hardie, Lord Advocate resigns. Colin Boyd, Solicitor General replaces him |
| March 1 | Scottish Parliament votes 63-59 to endorse the Executive's local government spending settlement |
| March 10 | Tony Blair, Prime Minister addresses the Scottish Parliament |
| March 16 | Conservatives win the Scottish Parliament by-election at Ayr from Labour turning a Labour majority of 25 into a Tory one of 3,344 |
| March 20 | Budget (Scotland) Act receives Royal Assent |
| March 28 | Brian Souter announces his intention to fund an unofficial referendum on the Executive's plan to abolish Section 28 |
| March 29 | Adults with Incapacity Bill passes all parliamentary stages |
| April 5 | Parliament approves amended Holyrood Building Plans of £195 million by 67-58 votes |

a new politics?

| April 27 | Tommy Sheridan's Abolition of Poindings and Warrant Sales Bill passed 79 to 15 with 30 abstentions; General principle of Ethical Standards in Public Life etc (Scotland) Bill including repeal of Section 28 passed 103 to 16 |
|---|---|
| May 3 | Abolition of Feudal Tenure Bill passes all parliamentary stages |
| May 8 | Donald Dewar undergoes heart surgery; Jim Wallace deputises as First Minister |
| May 9 | Adults with Incapacity Act receives Royal Assent |
| May 11 | Scottish Executive announces statutory backing for sex education guidance for teachers |
| May 18 | UK Home Secretary Jack Straw agrees entry to UK for boxer Mike Tyson to fight in Scotland |
| May 30 | Unofficial referendum on Section 28 shows 86.8 per cent opposition to repeal on a 34.5 per cent turnout |

Source: authors data; GPC Scotland

## Table 2: A Chronology of UK Devolution

**1998:**

| May 22 | Good Friday Agreement endorsed by referendum |
|---|---|
| June 25 | Northern Ireland Assembly Elections |
| July 1 | David Trimble elected First Minister and Seamus Mallon Deputy First Minister |
| Sept. 19 | Ron Davies defeats Rhodri Morgan for the post of Welsh Labour leader |
| Oct. 30 | Ron Davies resigns as Welsh leader after his walk on Clapman Common |

**1999:**

Feb. 20     Alun Michael narrowly defeats Rhodri Morgan as Welsh Labour leader

May 12      Alun Michael elected First Secretary; Welsh Executive nominated of seven ministers

July 1      National Assembly for Wales formally opened

July 28     Paul Murphy becomes Secretary of State for Wales

Oct. 11     Peter Mandelson becomes Northern Ireland Secretary

Nov. 29     Nomination of 10 Northern Irish ministers under d'Hondt rule completing Executive of 12 with First and Deputy First Minister

Dec. 2      Power transferred to Northern Ireland Assembly and Executive has first meeting

**2000:**

Feb. 9      Alun Michael resigns as Welsh First Secretary; Labour lose vote of confidence 27-31

Feb. 11     Peter Mandelson suspends Northern Ireland Assembly after 72 days of devolution

Feb. 15     Rhodri Morgan becomes Welsh First Secretary

Feb. 20     Frank Dobson narrowly defeats Ken Livingstone for the Labour candidate for London Mayor

March 6     Ken Livingstone announces his Independent candidature for Mayor

May 4       Ken Livingstone wins election as London Mayor as an Independent candidate

May 6       IRA announces it is prepared to put its arms 'beyond use'

a new politics?

| May 27 | Peter Mandelson signs the order devolving power |
| May 30 | Devolution restored to Northern Ireland; Ministers take their places in power-sharing Executive |

Sources: Northern Irish dates, Robin Wilson, Democratic Dialogue; Welsh figures, Leighton Andrews, Welsh Context

ENDNOTE:
(1) All figures are for MSPs elected in the 1999 Scottish Parliament elections and MPs elected in 1997 and exclusive by-elections held since.

# SECTION 1 the changing scottish political environment

# CHAPTER 2: scotland year zero: the first year at holyrood

## iain macwhirter

Well, no one can say it has been boring. In fact, the Scottish Parliament has got off to a cracking start, fulfilling its promise to bring Parliament closer to the people, passing long overdue legislation, holding public figures and institutions to account, reviving democratic participation and mobilising the intellectual and social capital of the Scottish people. In only twelve months Holyrood has established itself as the central focus of national life in Scotland. It is impossible to think of Scotland without her Parliament.

Mind you, say all that in the company of any given group of Scottish citizens and you are likely to get a rather sharp response. I know; I have done it. They are liable to react as if you have been living on another planet. The planet Holyrood, as we all know, has been an assembly of no-hope numpties, who spend their time arguing about expenses when they are not off on holiday. The popular view of the Scottish Parliament is that it has been an embarrassing shambles: at best a waste of public money, at worst a translation of 'coonoil' sleaze into national politics. Far from reviving respect for politicians, the wrangling over the coalition between Labour and the Liberal Democrats has induced even more public cynicism, and the spiralling cost of the new Parliament's building has made Holyrood a national disgrace before it is built.

So we end the first year of the new Scottish democracy with two contradictory accounts - a constitutional schizophrenia which, come to think of it, corresponds rather well to our national ambivalence towards Scottish identity and national life. So, which assessment is right? I would tend to the former, but would have to accept that elements of the latter are undeniably true.

# THE JEKYLL AND HYDE PARLIAMENT

Perhaps it is a Jekyll and Hyde Parliament that we have on the Mound, which seems at once to be a great leap forward for Scottish democracy and a step back into the mire of parochialism. The 'Jekyll Parliament' is all about legislation, procedure, scrutiny - all the abstract qualities which the lumpen Scot dismisses as 'pointy-headed'. The 'Hyde Parliament' expresses the empty-headed cronyism that has dominated local government in West Central Scotland and which seeks to mould Holyrood in the image of South Lanarkshire Council.

The Jekyllite tendency recognises that a Parliament starting from scratch, elected under proportional representation with inexperienced legislators and radically new procedures, was bound to have a difficult time learning its craft under the relentless glare of an often hostile media. It credits the Scottish Parliament with having introduced a range of long-overdue legislation, from land reform to the abolition of warrant sales; from the Adults with Incapacity Bill to the repeal of Section 28 (well, nearly). The committee system of the new Parliament has more then matched expectations, with pre-legislative committees such as Justice and Enterprise already establishing themselves as powerful instruments of scrutiny and propagators of policy. The main problem has been legislative overload. Attempts by lobbyists to infect the Parliament early with sleaze were seen off early by the Standards Committee in a confrontation with the Executive in September which established an important precedent in the eternal battle between Parliament and Executive.

But the 'Hyde Parliament', by contrast, is all about incompetent backbenchers who can barely read their planted questions, let alone mount a coherent argument in debate. It is a Parliament which could not even take responsibility for its own building, and has allowed the cost to overrun by four times, without anyone being held to account. It is a Parliament with so little sense of its own authority that it needs Tony Blair to come north to see off Brian Souter and his kailyard fundamentalists over Section 28.

In the 'Hyde Parliament', cliques of inarticulate ex-councilors spend their days 'fixing' issues using the numpty networks of old Labour, while anyone capable of joined-up thinking is frozen out. It is the Parliament of philistines which regards culture as suspect and whose first act, when the Holyrood Building scandal broke, was to axe the art budget. It is the Parliament of Ministers so keen on currying favour with the *Daily Record*, that they are prepared to abandon collective cabinet responsibility in their efforts to appease Anderston Quay.

# THE PAPER LIONS OF THE SCOTTISH PRESS AND SECTION 28

It is of course impossible to discuss Scotland Year Zero without taking into account the malign media climate into which this Parliament was born. The Hyde tendency is partly a response to the kind of poisonous coverage to which the Parliament has been subjected by the Scottish tabloids. The real nightmare on Holyrood is that the Scottish Parliament might one day take on the outlook and attitudes of the Scottish political press corps in their Lawnmarket warren. And will the last person to leave Scotland please turn out the light.

From day one, the Scottish popular press has been determined that devolution shall not succeed, at least not as an exercise in civilised government. The *Record*, under its editor Martin Clarke, has led a sustained campaign of misrepresentation and vilification which has created a cartoon image of a Parliament of fools and charlatans which has entered popular mythology. First it was the canard that MSPs paid themselves '£86,000 in pay and perks'. This inflated remuneration was calculated by adding MSPs' office allowances to their salaries, as if the computer used by a researcher was part of the MSP's pay. Then they claimed that MSPs were taking seventeen weeks holiday, when, of course, they were working in their constituencies during most of the parliamentary recess. The nadir was the medallions affair, when the *Record* attacked MSPs for awarding themselves commemorative medals (they were not but never mind) to mark the state opening of the Scottish Parliament. War veterans were interviewed expressing their outrage at MSPs pinning medals on their chests for doing nothing at all.

Of course, some of it was fun - though it was rarely harmless. Sir David Steel, the Presiding Officer, tried to respond in kind by attacking the *Record* for peddling 'bitch journalism' and referring them to the Press Complaints Commission (PCC). The PCC sided with Anderston Quay.

The *Record's* campaign took a sinister turn in December when the scandal broke over the Head of the Executive Policy Unit, John Rafferty. After allegations that he had briefed journalists that the Health Minister, Susan Deacon, had received death threats, Rafferty was forced to resign. It was the beginning of Donald Dewar's winter of discontent. The *Record* exposed the late night visits of another of Dewar's special advisers in a Glasgow red-light area. He had to go, leaving the Policy Unit leaderless, under strength, and demoralised.

In the New Year, the *Record* threw its not inconsiderable weight behind Brian Souter's campaign to keep Section 28 (or Clause 2A as it should be in Scotland) on the promotion of homosexuality in schools. Working in concert now with the *Scottish Daily Mail* and the *Scottish Sun*, the Glasgow tabloid mounted one of the most disgraceful newspaper campaigns ever seen in Britain, claiming that homosexual groups were planning to flood schools with homosexual propaganda if and when the Executive scrapped Section 28. It outrageously accused the Executive of advocating 'gay sex lessons' in Scottish classrooms. The Communities Minister, Wendy Alexander, was pilloried as an out-of-touch feminist harpie, obsessed with politically correct gesture politics. Cardinal Winning was given star treatment, and applauded for calling homosexual acts 'perverted'. The *Record* also backed his attacks on the Health Minister Susan Deacon, whose advocacy of sex education for teenage girls was called, 'promoting easy sex'.

Clause 2A came to dominate the thoughts of Ministers. Instead of concentrating on more important issues - Parliament had voted massively for repeal of Clause 2A - some of them tried to bounced the Scottish government into abandoning its policy. The 'Three Wise Men' as the *Record* put it. This episode almost split the coalition, and only determined opposition in the Scottish Labour group of MSPs prevented the policy from descending into chaos.

However, under pressure from the private ballot organised by Brian Souter, the policy again became unstable in May 2000 and Sam Galbraith, Education Minister announced future guidance to local authorities on sex education would be made legally binding. He insisted that this did not mean that the guidelines on sex education in schools had been put on a statutory basis. However, it was clear to the SNP, whose policy this had been all along and to the Lib Dems, who were party to the new policy change that the guidelines could not be separated from the guidance and that this was merely a semantic distinction designed to save the Executive and in particular, Sam Galbraith's face.

The entire Clause 2A affair was a media-inspired campaign of disinformation, but the Parliament's response to it betrayed a deep insecurity among MSPs about their role, powers, and standing in Scottish society. Perhaps, after being denigrated for months, it was hardly surprising that they should have lost self-confidence - at least on the Labour benches, where they continue to take the *Record* far more seriously than it merits. It is of course MSPs who possess the democratic mandate, not the *Record*; it is Parliament that makes the laws, not Anderston Quay; it is Donald Dewar who is First Minister, not Cardinal Winning.

But an inexperienced Parliament was paralysed by the affair, frozen in the lights. Too many MSPs, especially on the Labour benches, do not seem to really know what they are there for; do not fully comprehend the responsibilities and powers that go along with their public office.

It is not yet clear how the Clause 2A affair will end, although there is little doubt that the clause will be scrapped in Scotland before it is repealed in England. The lack of a revising chamber like the House of Lords to focus moral reaction, has meant that there is no legislative barrier to the repeal legislation reaching the statute book this summer. But it is arguable that, without the partnership with the Liberal Democrats, it might never have got there intact.

## THE POLITICS OF PARTNERSHIP

The coalition has had almost as bad a press as the repeal of Section 28. The negotiations of the Partnership Agreement last summer was reported as unprincipled wheeler-dealing, designed to distribute ministerial Mondeos. While the tabloids attacked the Lib Dems for selling out, and Labour for letting them in, the actual terms of the coalition deal were largely ignored. But not only did they ensure that university tuition fees would be abolished, they also ensured that the Scottish Freedom of Information Bill would be a more liberal measure than the Jack Straw equivalent in Whitehall. The Partnership Agreement, also provided for the reform of the system of judicial appointment, which seemed highly technical at the time, but became a matter of huge public interest after the resignation of the Lord Advocate, Lord Hardie, and his awarding himself a position on the bench. It also provided for electoral reform in local government and the setting up of the Kerley Inquiry into electoral methods. We await the Kerley Report, as I write, but the Liberal Democrats are determined that proportional representation will happen.

There could be no more dramatic illustration of the success of the new politics. Here we have coalition, consensus politics for the first time anywhere on the British mainland - and it is actually working. The Cubie Report into university funding was a model of co-operative politics, which managed to express a real national consensus on student grants, even if it was not implemented to the letter. The new politics is forging a new political landscape in Scotland, from the committees of the Parliament to the one-party states of West Central Scotland. Anyone who looks objectively at the achievements of the Scottish Parliament in its first year would have to conclude that it has had a major impact on Scottish civil society.

But do not expect the Hyde tendency to recognise it. The animus of the Scottish press toward the institution is so intense, that electoral reform is liable to be dismissed as yet more politically correct nonsense, undermining the authority of local administrations, and leading to compromise and deadlock in town halls across Scotland. A majority of Labour MSPs probably oppose electoral reform.

The essential problem with the media coverage of Holyrood has been an inability to distinguish between the fortunes of the Scottish Parliament and the fortunes of the Labour-led administration. When there is turbulence in London government it is seen as a problem for Labour; when there is trouble in the Scottish coalition, it is seen as crisis in Scottish democracy. When Labour advisers such as Charlie Whelan or Peter Mandelson resign, it is seen as Tony Blair's problem; when Scottish special advisers resign, it is seen as a crisis for the Scottish Parliament. Everything, from the mishandling of the Holyrood Building contract to the activities of Beattie Media, is presented as indications that devolution is not working. This attitude has been apparent even in the broadsheet coverage of the Parliament's first year. The *Scotsman* even blamed devolution for the state of Scottish rugby.

You can only conclude that Scottish journalists and editors do not really understand the nature of the institution they are reporting. In fact, many of the so called 'parliamentary crises' are actually indications of its success - such as the 'Lobbygate' hearings. Even Section 28, in a perverse way, is an indication of the way Holyrood has galvanised public debate in Scotland. It has exposed the strand of social conservatism which has been latent in West Central Scottish politics for years.

What has not happened is the slippery slope to independence. Opponents of devolution said that a Scottish Parliament would only benefit the Scottish National Party and hasten the disintegration of the UK. It is too early, of course, to pronounce on that thesis - but what we can say, after one year of Holyrood, is that the Parliament has not provided the platform for nationalist demagogues that many expected. Far from it. Indeed, the SNP has been on the sidelines of politics for long periods, as the dynamics of the coalition worked themselves out through the long winter months of serial crisis. The Parliament has not become a megaphone demanding cash with menaces from Westminster. Indeed, Scotland seems to have stopped blaming London for everything that is wrong in Scottish society. They now have someone else to blame in Edinburgh. If you like, the grievance culture has been repatriated: instead of girning about Westminster, Scots are now girning about the Scottish Parliament.

This has been most striking over finance and the Barnett Formula. The controversial formula which calculates Scotland's share of annual increases in UK public spending has been applied with greater rigour under devolution than ever before in its twenty two year life. As a result, Scottish spending is set to rise by considerably less, proportionately, in the coming years than was ever the case under the Tories. In particular, the six per cent year on year increase promised by the Prime Minister for health spending will not apply in Scotland, where under Barnett this will be nearer five per cent. But despite determined efforts by the SNP to alert Scotland to the impact of the 'Barnett Squeeze', there has been little or no public outcry. The Health Minister Susan Deacon merely observed that, since Scotland already gets 20 per cent more per head, we could not expect to get the same proportionate increase as England.

This is surely a remarkable development - a nation actually electing to be less well off. Perhaps, once the spending starts to feed through, there will be more complaints about Scotland not getting her six per cent, but so far there is no sign of it. Call it maturity, call it ignorance - but the annual gripe about the Scottish block grant settlement has not happened this year. Instead, the debate about spending has been confined to how the £16bn Scottish budget should be distributed - led by Donald Dewar, who has invited Scots to contribute to the debate.

It is a victory, of sorts, for the Tartan Tax. No party has called for the Parliament's power to vary income tax by three pence in the pound to be used - though the SNP wanted to forego the penny tax cut in Chancellor Brown's 1999 budget. It seems that the much-maligned tax power has concentrated minds in Scotland. It is one thing demanding more spending from Westminster, it is quite another raising Scottish taxes to pay for it. It seems that Scotland is not that different after all.

Again, this is surely a tribute to the success of the Scottish Parliament. If it has abolished the 'Scottish whinge' (if not the 'Scottish cringe') then all to the good. If the experience of the Holyrood Building project has brought a new fiscal realism into public debate north of the Border, and impressed upon Scots the importance of living within your means, then this too is surely a good lesson for an infant Parliament to learn. The Parliament has brought the kind of cultural revolution the Tories would have been proud to call their own, had it not been for the fact that they have disowned devolution (which, of course, was originally proposed by the Conservative Prime Minister, Edward Heath, in 1968).

Instead, it is left to new Labour to claim credit for 'modernising' Scottish politics, and ending the politics of dependency. The trouble is, however, that while Labour might have been the agency of the revolution, it is still possible that they could be consumed by it. The SNP has changed too, within the Parliament, from a party of protest, to a party aspiring to run Holyrood on its own terms. Alex Salmond is playing the role of Her Majesty's Opposition, and playing it rather well. If Labour does not get its act together, stop fearing the *Record* and learn how to be a proper government, we could be seeing a nationalist leadership on the Mound rather sooner than anyone expected.

# CHAPTER 3: the challenge to the parties: institutions, ideas and strategies

## james mitchell

The challenges and opportunities offered by devolution to Scotland's political parties are becoming clear one year after the establishment of the Parliament. These can be categorised under three headings: institutions, ideas and strategies. Each party is having to adapt its internal institutions to take account of devolution, develop new political ideas and devise new electoral strategies. Scottish politics has become more complex with more dimensions than was the case in the past. Each party faces new challenges but equally each has a new opportunity to make its mark on Scotland.

## INSTITUTIONS

The new public institutions created by devolution - the Parliament and its committees, the electoral system, and the slowly evolving intergovernmental machinery - have all required some parallel innovations within each of the parties. Some greater autonomy for the Scottish parties was inevitable, whether formally or informally, after devolution. Each party now chooses its own Scottish leader. Donald Dewar, David McLetchie and Jim Wallace can all claim to have the backing of their parties in Scotland. That does not mean that each party has internally devolved power equally. The extent to which the Scottish Labour Party is allowed to choose its own leader has yet to become clear. Donald Dewar's coronation was the result of the happy coincidence of London and Scotland wanting the same thing. The test of devolution will only occur when London and Scotland are in dispute. As London and Wales have shown, new Labour has devolved state institutions but has yet to accept the need to devolve itself in these places. Formal devolution may have occurred but within a centralised mind set.

It was inevitable that Labour, as the governing party, would face more challenges than the other parties. Part of the problem arises because of the nature of the devolution 'settlement' (devolution is far from settled). The retention of the office of Secretary of State has created unnecessary tensions. The failure of devolutionists to pay serious attention to the London-Edinburgh relationship prior to 1997 has resulted in both the First Minister and the Secretary of State competing for authority in formal government and internal party politics. It is probably only a matter of time before the office of Secretary of State for Scotland is abolished. So long as it exists there will continue to be heated and damaging clashes with implications not only for government but also for internal Labour Party politics.

Curiously, Scottish Labour Action (SLA) disbanded before it had achieved all it set out to do. It may well be that SLA activists concluded that Scottish party autonomy, which had been a key objective, would follow devolution. To some extent that is proving correct but whether the form party autonomy takes is quite what was envisaged is another matter. Modernisation is an amazingly elastic term in new Labour discourse: modernisation of the party means increased central control while modernisation of the state means more decentralisation. Party institutions have been denuded of power. Scottish conference may develop more autonomy in relation to the British conference but as the latter is a happy-clappy gathering this means very little.

The SNP is also coming to terms with devolution. The organisation and structure of the party evolved in an ad hoc manner, much in the same way as the British constitution. Its membership has considerable input into decision-making with national conference and national council having real power. Lessons from the 1970s when it had eleven MPs, at Westminster who were often at war with the national executive have not been fully taken on board. There are obvious differences with that time, not least that Alex Salmond is leader of the party and the group of SNP MSPs, and there is not the same distance - geographically or culturally - between those elected by the party and those elected by the public. Nonetheless, the group of MSPs has become the public face of the party. In effect, power has shifted towards this group without any corresponding changes in the formal institutions of the party. Beefing up the formal party decision-making forums would only create the kind of tensions which did so much damage to the SNP in the 1970s. Coming to terms with the fact that the SNP is now a parliamentary party in an age of professional politics means that the SNP will have to confront its outmoded decision-making processes. That will be strongly resisted in a party which, despite its constitutional radicalism, is very conservative when it comes to its internal constitution.

# IDEAS

The challenge facing all parties is to convince Scots that the Parliament fills more than an emotive hole. Throughout the years of Conservative rule, the non-Tory parties did not worry too much about policy-making and developing ideas for government. Even new Labour, for all its emphasis on being seen as a party fit for government, concentrated on ditching potentially unpopular policies rather than developing new policies. It moved from aspirational, idealistic politics (or uncosted irresponsible politics depending on viewpoint) to sloganising - from 'stakeholding' to the 'Third Way'. The SNP seems to be slowly moving in this direction too. The SNP has changed its watchword from 'Scotland First' to 'Safety First'. The non-Tory parties are all capable of governing Scotland. None would create the mayhem that its opponents claim but each fears that it will be branded as irresponsible. The consequence of this is that policy-making conservatism has won out by default.

The constraints placed on imaginative policy making within the parties have been imposed by electoral fears. It is ironic that this ideological straitjacket has been imposed at the very moment in Scottish history when new institutions were established which promised to open up policy making. Scrape away the rhetoric of 'newness' and a lot is very familiar. In some policy areas, some radical new thinking is emerging. Of course, any radical new policy is bound to be treated with suspicion and a combination of vested interests and genuinely fearful groups can usually mobilized against the best policies. The proposals for urban governance in Glasgow may prove a major exception to the rule. Two features of the proposals stand out. The full impact of the proposals will not be fully felt for a long time. There is opposition to them from people who are understandably suspicious of yet another experiment promising much and appear suspiciously like a way of ditching a problem rather than confronting it. These features should not condemn the proposals but, assuming for a moment that they are clearly thought out and will indeed deliver what is promised of them, should commend themselves to anyone determined to break out of the cycle of blame and despondency which has characterised Scottish urban policy. If, however, these proposals turn out to be a way of devolving penury - the Scottish Executive dumping a dreadful set of problems - then they would amount to an act of extraordinary cynicism and raise questions about the constitutional 'settlement'. Given the electoral base of Labour, much may rest on Wendy Alexander's initiative.

A feature of policy-making in the past was that only a small number of initiatives were possible in any one Parliament - ministerial and parliamentary time were just not available. There is no such excuse with the Scottish Parliament. The degree of innovation is patchy across the range of the Parliament's responsibilities especially compared with what has been coming out of London since 1997. Perhaps this is deliberate but it is more that this reflects ministerial abilities.

## STRATEGIES

When it comes to strategy, the party in most need of help is the Liberal Democrat Party. It is now suffering from a loss of identity through association with Labour. To ask Liberal Democrats to explain what the party stands for can result in a detailed, sometimes informed exposition but trying to capture it in a way that could be sold to the electorate seems beyond them. The image as a 'moderate', 'sensible' party is not enough - especially given the crowded field of parties making this claim. Having failed to cut out a clear programme for government which they could call their own, Liberal Democrats are being used by Labour, with remarkable ease, as the fall guys. It may not be working to Labour's advantage as well as its strategists had hoped, but there is no doubt that letting the Liberal Democrats make unpopular announcements is damaging Scotland's fourth party. Each of the other parties must be eyeing the Liberal Democrat vote greedily. This most disparate vote is up for grabs and the next election may hinge on where it goes.

The Tories are no longer looking over the abyss. The only question that should be asked about David McLetchie's leadership is why did the Tories not give him the job much earlier. He has the advantage of building his party without the glare of media attention, something that Hague does not have. But even accounting for that, he and his party have made considerable progress. The occasional potshot at the leadership in London is as much about redefining the party as was its 'Scotland First' Scottish manifesto. His troops in the Scottish Parliament appear more comfortable there than they should be for a party which fought almost to the death to oppose it coming into being, but McLetchie can probably rely on the short-term memory of the electorate to help him redefine his party's image. As a party, the Tories seem more at ease with devolution than does new Labour. McLetchie is in the process of returning his party to its roots.

The SNP's most immediate problem will be the UK general election. Not because, as Labour insists, the SNP do not have a role there (if they do not then neither does Labour) but because its candidates will all be fairly inexperienced. None of those it can expect to see elected will have much idea about the Commons or its procedures. More important will be the strategy for future Scottish elections. The Salmond strategy is fairly clear and without doubt is the party's best hope. Taking a leaf out of new Labour's book, the SNP is positioning itself as a party of the responsible left. It wants to appeal to disaffected Labour voters, who hold the key to an SNP breakthrough, while not provoking a well-funded establishment onslaught. The problem is that the establishment onslaught will happen whatever the SNP says or does. The SNP leadership knows this but are determined that they do not hand their opponents any more weapons. As the Scottish election campaign showed, the SNP had difficulty enough contending with the scares that were dreamt up by their opponents without having to contend with any of their own making. Salmond and the SNP will have to devise a strategy for dealing with scare stories and vicious personalised attacks. Labour did this by abandoning much that it believed in but the SNP cannot and will not do that. Independence is a much firmer SNP commitment than socialism ever was for Labour.

Salmond's other problem is keeping his party on message and preventing the odd balls from undermining what he has achieved. Party management has always been more difficult in the SNP given its constitution and structure than any other party. Salmond is, by far, the SNP's greatest asset and its best leader and his party knows it. Daft reports in Labour-supporting newspapers that he will face a challenge appear periodically. There are no serious challengers on the horizon but that does not mean that he is free of trouble. Salmond's challenge comes from a few malcontents who will always be given space in the media to attack him. The party members probably find this as irritating as the leadership and may prove more amenable to internal constitutional changes which would strengthen the institutional power of the leadership. It would be a gamble to set out on this course and the timing would be important but there seems little doubt that an SNP breakthrough will only come after the party is organised as a potential party of government and not a party of protest.

Labour's most pressing needs appear contradictory: it needs to appear more united and more disunited simultaneously. The lack of unity in the Executive has not yet reached levels which should cause too much concern but the race to succeed Donald Dewar is becoming intense. Even if Dewar remains First Minister for another decade the jockeying has started and will only end when a successor is finally chosen. The contest to succeed Dewar will tell us much about the future course of Scottish politics. Under Dewar, Scottish Labour has had a honeymoon - it may not always seem that way for the party but that is how it will be seen in the future. Whoever succeeds Dewar will have none of his personal authority and standing. One issue which will be important will be how candidates view the relationship between London and Edinburgh. In this respect, Scottish Labour is in danger of being too united. It is always more difficult for a party of government, but Labour in Scotland cannot afford not to be seen to be in dispute with London occasionally - and winning. If the battle becomes a Scottish version of the Brown-Blair tension then that will only do the party more damage.

A major battle is looming not far in the future which will affect Labour more than any other party. As Ken Livingstone has made clear, Scotland's share of public spending is no longer sacrosanct. The issue of territorial shares of public spending is going to become a test of Labour's skill. Whatever 'solution' is found it will be one firmly rooted in political compromise rather than a well worked out technical exercise. Scottish Labour will have to be seen to have fought its corner powerfully and effectively. Other parts of the UK will be trying to do likewise and Labour at the centre will be trying to choreograph it all so that each local party appears to have won something. To achieve that will be no mean feat. This is the essence of the challenge Labour faces. As a devolutionist party in government, it has the unenviable task of balancing competing demands, but allowing each local party to appear victorious. Finance is probably the most significant issue which can be seen on the horizon but it will not be the only one. Other unforeseen problems of this type will come along and will need careful handling.

## CONCLUSION

It would be wrong to concentrate only on the difficulties which devolution brings. Devolution offers each an opportunity. The Tories have a chance in the comfort of opposition to redefine and rebuild themselves. As David McLetchie has shown, devolution offers a new political space in which the party can reassert its Scottishness. The Liberal Democrats have more pressures than opportunities but they too can take advantage of being part of government to claim they now have some authority and government experience. Consolidation is central for this party of local heroes. They are vulnerable given the lack of a 'corporate image'. The platform offered by government gives them an opportunity to project a clearer corporate image.

Devolution is potentially the single most important event in the history of the SNP. It now has the opportunity to become a party of government. It needs to shed its eccentric, often divided image. Party members have indulged some fringe figures in the past but will require to be more disciplined if they want to take the next step forward. The problem for the SNP is that while Alex Salmond may be the most impressive party leader in Scotland - the kind Scottish Labour needs - his party is not built in his image.

Internal Scottish unity alongside creative conflict within the party in Britain is proving more difficult than it should for Labour. It may take a change in the leadership in London, or at least a change of attitude there, but Labour cannot afford to operate as if the UK is a unitary state. When Labour as a party comes to terms with devolution, it has a better chance of ensuring that devolution is indeed the settled will of the Scottish people and in so doing maintaining its position as Scotland's largest party. As the devolutionist party, Labour needs to come to terms with its own policy. When it does that, then it might just succeed in making devolution the 'settled will of the Scottish people'.

# the holyrood project

## janice kirkpatrick

The first year of the Scottish Parliament was more of a refresher course in how to be 'professionally Scottish'. We were all called upon to be all that the world expected Scots to be - brave, innovative, cosmopolitan and capable of making shrewd investments in the future of our Nation.

We had the strength and foresight to commission a superlative backdrop for the business of government, an architectural asset that will project the impression of an international and ambitious Scotland around the globe. In true Scottish fashion we soldiered bravely on against a makeshift backdrop of borrowed council chambers and building sites before finally losing our nerve, and the international vote of confidence we had worked so hard to win.

We bickered over the cost of the project rather than understanding its true value. We embarrassingly revealed our amateurism and parochialism by expecting to build our Parliament for less than the price of a shopping mall then rudely berating the architect for not being Scottish, whatever that means in our multicultural society.

In 1950 Hugh MacDiarmid said :

> *The mass of the people will react all right if they get the chance. It is the stupid conservatism of their self-styled betters that's the danger. Amateurism has always been the curse of the arts in Scotland - amateurism and the inveterate predilection to 'domesticate the issue'.*

I think it was Winston Churchill who said 'We shape our buildings: thereafter they shape us.' Maybe the architecture should have come before the MSPs.

# CHAPTER 4:  the new electoral politics

## john curtice

Elections are at the heart of legislative devolution. In creating a Scottish Parliament, the proponents of devolution wanted to create a body that could do things differently from Westminster. They thus reasoned that Scotland needed a body whose mandate was entirely separate from that of the Westminster Parliament. And to help ensure the new Parliament would indeed be something different from Westminster, they also endowed it with a new electoral system.

But some proponents of devolution at least also had another aim. This was to put the nationalist genie back into the bottle. By granting Scotland devolution the UK Parliament would demonstrate that the hopes and aspirations of Scots could be fulfilled within the framework of the Union. As a result, demands for independence would disappear and support for the SNP wither.

It has not all turned out as intended. True, many of the hopes of devolutionists have been fulfilled. But this has only happened because, far from withering on the devolution vine, support for the SNP has flourished in the new electoral context. As a result it is far from clear that the introduction of devolution has finally settled the constitutional debate in Scotland.

## THE SEPARATE MANDATE

There was never any guarantee that devolution would make a difference. After all, local councils have long had their own elections. Yet this has done little to stop central government increasingly encroaching on their powers. Unfortunately for local government, far fewer people vote in local elections than in Westminster elections, while many of those that do vote decide how to do so on the basis of what is going on centrally rather than locally. As a result elections do not give local government the authority to say to central government, 'Whatever you think is best, this is what we have been elected to do'. Central government, however, is often reliant on the performance of local government to achieve what it has promised the electorate, such as better schools or new roads. Little wonder that the autonomy of local councils has been squeezed.

So in order for the new Parliament to be effective, voters needed first of all to be persuaded to come to the polls. Moreover, when they did so they needed to cast their vote on the basis of the issues confronting the Scottish Parliament rather than the current strengths and weaknesses of the UK government at Westminster. Above all, they need to be prepared to vote differently from how they might have done so in a Westminster election.

None of these things could be relied upon, especially in the very first Scottish election. After all voters were being asked to vote for a new institution whose importance and impact on their lives was far from clear, and which had no past record upon which it could be judged. The election campaign took place in the midst of British involvement in a war in Kosovo. And the Labour Party at least fought an election campaign which emphasised the virtues of what it had achieved in office as the UK government, implying that the policy of the new Scottish Parliament should be along similar lines. It was almost as though Labour were inviting Scots to choose on the basis of what was going on at Westminster.

## THE NEW ELECTORAL SYSTEM

On the other hand there was one feature of the Scottish election that might help encourage voters to behave differently. This was the introduction of a new electoral system. A variant of the Additional Member System used in Germany and New Zealand, the new system still required voters to vote for a local representative for their Westminster constituency. But at the same time they had a second vote which could be cast for a regional party list. These second votes would be used to determine the allocation of 56 extra seats, such that the combined total of constituency and list seats in each of the eight regions was proportional to the distribution of the second vote.

The new system thus gave voters new opportunities, not least the ability to vote for a different party on the two ballots. But it also perhaps ran the risk of confusion. Proportional representation is after all often associated in the public mind with complexity. Perhaps all that having a new system would do is make it less likely that voters would turn out at all.

the new electoral politics

# THE NATIONALIST GENIE

Devolution first entered the lexicon of Scottish and British politics after the SNP's first ever parliamentary victory in the 1967 Hamilton by-election. The first attempts to legislate for its introduction came after the SNP won 30 per cent of the vote in the October 1974 general election. And devolution burst into new life in the form of the Scottish Constitutional Convention after another spectacular SNP victory in Govan in 1988.

In short, devolution is a response to nationalist success. By giving Scotland relative autonomy within the UK, it was hoped this success might be reversed. Yet by the time that the first Scottish Parliament election took place a fundamental change had happened in Scottish politics. The SNP had clearly replaced the Conservatives as the principal opposition party to Labour in Scotland, a feat it had not achieved in the 1970s. In every election after 1992, be it local, European or Westminster, the SNP outpolled the Conservatives. True, thanks to the quirks of the first past the post electoral system, the SNP remained behind the Liberal Democrats in terms of seats in the 1997 general election, but even so it was still the nationalists who were second to Labour in most constituencies in Scotland. And above all, there was little sign of any Tory revival by the time of the first Scottish election.

As a result, far from being a threat to the future of the SNP the first Scottish election appeared to be an opportunity. If voters were dissatisfied with the performance of the UK government and wanted to use the Scottish election as a chance to express their views, then voting SNP would seem the most effective way of doing so. And whatever the basis on which voters decided to vote, the new electoral system should ensure that SNP strength was properly reflected in its parliamentary representation. In short, devolution appeared to give the party the chance to become a significant parliamentary force for the first time ever.

# THE OUTCOME

So how did the devolution settlement actually perform on its first electoral outing? So far as the turnout is concerned, the message appears to be rather mixed. 59 per cent of the electorate voted. This was well down on the 71 per cent who voted in the 1997 Westminster election, but was far higher than the 45 per cent who voted in the last round of Scottish local elections in 1995 or the 25 per cent who felt it worth casting a vote in the 1999 European election. Evidently while Scots felt that Holyrood mattered more than their local council or

Strasbourg, the election did not engage their interest to the degree that Westminster elections historically have done.

Evidence from the Scottish Parliamentary Election Study certainly suggests that Holyrood is widely considered to be important. For example, 56 per cent felt that the outcome of a Holyrood election mattered a 'great deal' or 'quite a lot', slightly higher in fact than the 54 per cent who said the same of Westminster. Moreover, those who felt that Holyrood mattered were more likely to vote in the first Scottish election (Curtice and Park, 2000). Indeed these figures may make one wonder why turnout in the first Holyrood election did not emulate previous Westminster turnouts. We should note however that this information was gathered immediately after a Scottish election but two years after the last Westminster one. Given how much more immediate a Scottish election was than a Westminster one, we might have expected more people to say that Holyrood mattered. On the other hand, we may discover that the advent of Holyrood will mean that some voters will no longer consider voting for Westminster, and that turnout in general elections in Scotland will be lower too.

What cannot account for the level of turnout is confusion about, or hostility to, the electoral system. In fact only 8 per cent of people in Scotland felt that the ballot papers were difficult to fill in (Curtice et al, 2000). True, far more, 40 per cent, felt that it was difficult to understand how the seats were allocated, But those who took that view were no less likely to vote in the election than those who did not. Equally, people's views for or against proportional representation made no apparent difference to their willingness to vote under the new system.

But what about those who did vote? Did they simply vote the same way that they would have done in a Westminster election? In truth, many did. The Scottish Parliamentary Election Study not only asked voters how they voted in the first Scottish election, but also how they would have voted in a Westminster election if one had been held the same day. No less than 82 per cent named as their Westminster choice the party that they said they had voted for on the first vote. The equivalent figure for the second vote is, at 76 per cent, only a little lower (Curtice and Steed, forthcoming 2000).

However, the decisions of those who did vote differently made a difference. The outcome of the first Scottish election was not the same as what would have happened in a Westminster election held on the same day. We can see this if we compare the distribution of Westminster preferences with the distribution of answers to a question on the Scottish Parliamentary Election Study which asked people to say who their first preference party was in the Scottish election (a distribution which in practice comes close to the actual outcome on the first vote). As the table below shows very clearly, Labour did significantly worse - and the SNP better - than would have been the case in a Westminster election.

## Table 3: Holyrood and Westminster Preferences 1999

|  | Holyrood 1st Preference (%) | Westminster Hypothetical Vote (%) | Difference (%) |
| --- | --- | --- | --- |
| Con | 16 | 16 | 0 |
| Lab | 39 | 48 | -9 |
| Lib Dem | 15 | 14 | +1 |
| SNP | 28 | 21 | +7 |

Source: Scottish Parliamentary Election Study 1999

So the mandate of the new Scottish Parliament does appear to be different from that of Westminster. But ironically that has only happened because, far from disappearing, the SNP thrived in the new electoral arena created by devolution (see Table 4 for full Scottish Parliament results). It is a pattern that shows every sign of maintaining itself. Throughout the first year of the new Parliament, System Three has regularly found that more people say that they would vote SNP in a Scottish election than would do so in a Westminster one. Thus on the first anniversary of the new Parliament the SNP at 35% on the first vote and 31% on the second vote, was actually one point ahead of Labour while, when it came to Westminster intentions, Labour retained a lead of 18 points.

## Table 4: Scottish Parliament Election Results 1999

|  | 1997 | 1999 First Vote | Change since 1997 | Second Vote | Change since 1997 |
| --- | --- | --- | --- | --- | --- |
| Labour | 45.6 | 38.8 | -6.8 | 33.6 | -12.0 |
| SNP | 22.1 | 28.7 | +6.6 | 27.3 | +5.2 |
| Con | 17.5 | 15.5 | -2.0 | 15.4 | -2.1 |
| Libs | 13.0 | 14.2 | +1.2 | 12.4 | -0.6 |
| Others | 1.9 | 2.7 | +0.8 | 11.3 | +9.4 |

Devolution has helped the SNP genie shine more brightly than ever. Why however did this happen? Does it reflect people's views on the policies and priorities of the new Parliament, as devolutionists might hope? In truth, this does not appear to be the case. People's views about the two domestic issues that dominated the 1999 election campaign do not appear to account for the reluctance of some Labour Westminster supporters to back the party for Holyrood, or for the willingness of some voters to back the SNP for Holyrood when it is not their choice for Westminster. For example, over two in five of Labour's Westminster supporters opposed the introduction of university tuition fees, but the percentage of these who failed to turn out and support Labour in the Scottish election is, at 42 per cent, little different from the 35 per cent of those who supported tuition fees (Curtice and Park, 2000).

On the other hand, there is no evidence that voters were using the SNP as a vehicle to express a mid-term protest against the performance of the UK government. Rather, the SNP's advantage appears to be more deep seated, reflecting the electorate's perceptions about who might best use the new institution to stand up for Scotland's interests. For example, only 8 per cent of voters, including just 15 per cent of Labour Westminster supporters, always trust the party to work in Scotland's interests. In contrast, no less than one in four of all Scots always trust the SNP. These perceptions made a difference. Those Westminster Labour supporters who did not trust their party to look after Scotland's interests were significantly less likely to back the party for Holyrood. Equally people who would not vote SNP in a Westminster election were more likely to turn to the party for Holyrood if they trusted the nationalists to advance Scotland's cause.

So the difference between the outcome of the first Scottish election and what would have happened in a Westminster election does not reflect Scots' views on what the new institution should do. To that degree the mandate of the first Scottish Parliament was perhaps not precisely the one that advocates of devolution were looking for. Rather it stemmed from views about who would best use Holyrood to advocate Scotland's case within the UK and beyond. And it was a criterion on which the SNP were able to score significantly more highly than their Labour opponents.

## CONCLUSION AND IMPLICATIONS

Three important implications flow from these findings. First, in contrast to local government, the Scottish Parliament does appear to have the electoral authority to do things differently from Westminster. It certainly seems to be expected to promote Scotland's distinctive interests in a way that Westminster is not. But, and this is our second implication, this poses a dilemma for any party that is already in power at Westminster. In a Scottish election any such party has to convince Scots that although it may share the same partisan label as the UK government, it will not be afraid to do things differently. For Labour, committed as it is to the benefits of staying 'on message', at all levels in the party, this has proven a particularly acute dilemma.

Finally, devolution has not settled the constitutional debate in Scotland. It has given the country an opposition that is committed to further constitutional change. Moreover, on the evidence of two by-elections held in the first year of the new Parliament, in Hamilton South and Ayr, that opposition is well placed to benefit if and when the Labour dominated administration becomes unpopular. Devolution has enabled the SNP to change from being a party of protest to a potential alternative government. If they are to stop that potential from being realised, Labour and the Liberal Democrats will have to prove that they can make Holyrood work to Scotland's advantage.

# social inclusion: one year on

## allan watt

'I used to call it poverty', said one contributor from the floor at a recent conference. He was referring to the new industry of social exclusion that has sprung up from the ashes of urban regeneration and anti-poverty policy. If you had not heard of social exclusion before 1997 you cannot miss it now. It has spawned a new network of policies across the UK and, perhaps rightly, reflects the fact that poverty is not a one dimensional issue.

Two years later, the Scottish Parliament picked up this issue and built a large part of its programme around it. Instead of the problem of social exclusion, the challenge of social inclusion has been built into the job description for our Minister for Communities and the title of her key committee. Targets have been published for the reduction of poverty but it has sometimes been hard to get a sense of the overall direction as specifics, such as the transfer of Glasgow's housing stock or abolition of warrant sales, dominate the headlines.

Therein lies the rub. Social inclusion cannot be achieved with one policy prescription but requires that every part of the Executive's legislative programme works towards it. At an early meeting of the Social Inclusion Committee, one member said: 'Our work is so wide-ranging that it would be easy for us to scratch at the surface of lots of issues related to poverty and the causes of poverty without actually achieving anything'. The press likes specific issues and since this issue cannot be neatly fitted into a box then, I suspect that few people would give our new Parliament much credit for its overall work so far.

A further issue raised early on in the committee was the central importance of employment and benefits legislation that are powers retained by Westminster. Few countries could expect to build a credible anti-poverty strategy without being able to change these crucial elements. The acid test for the Parliament is whether it can be convincing in bending such powers to deal with the Scottish situation and line them up with distinctive and radical Scottish policies in the areas that have been devolved.

# CHAPTER 5: rethinking representation: some evidence from the first year

**angela mccabe and james mccormick**

The new Parliament was established with a backward glance to history (the first to be directly elected for 300 years) as well as a focus on the future, and rooted in optimism about 'the new Scottish politics'. In the first year, critics have been quick to sow the seeds of doubt and disappointment. At times it has been hard to separate the words of the sceptic from those of the cynic and to agree upon real examples by which to test the added value of devolved government. Yet, the immediate reshaping of parliamentary representation arising from the new voting system brings into sharp focus some of the early effects of devolution.

This chapter draws on some of the early findings of a three-year study into the attitudes and behaviour of Scotland's new parliamentarians. It considers how the early experiences of MSPs compared with their initial expectations and in particular how they expected the roles of constituency and regional list members to develop.

In-depth interviews were conducted with thirteen MSPs in the period July-September 1999 (during the Parliament's recess). The panel comprises five constituency members and eight list members, including four 'dual mandate' members representing Westminster constituencies until the next UK election. It includes four of the parties represented in the Parliament. The panel has been supplemented with four other interviews, including academic commentators and one Scottish MP who represents a seat in England. The analysis presented here thus provides a snapshot of the early months of devolution.

## 'ALL MSPS ARE EQUAL BUT DIFFERENT'

The devolution legislation is silent on the relationships between elected members within the Scottish Parliament and between Holyrood and Westminster. Nor did the Consultative Steering Group (CSG) Code of Conduct

Working Group offer guidance on the issue. It stated that the relationships between MSPs and the public 'should be allowed to evolve in the light of experience' (Consultative Steering Group Working Group, 1999).

One of the first controversies of the Parliament, resulting in the Allowances Code of June 1999, raised questions about equality of status between the two types of member. While both constituency and list members have the same speaking rights in the chamber and the same formal rights of representation, they do not have the same level of allowances to carry out their representative roles. Each constituency member receives £10,000 each year to pay for a local office, while only the first-elected member of each party's regional list receives the same amount. Thereafter, list members of the same party receive only £3,000 per year, with implications for how list MSPs cover the regions they are elected to serve. This has led some MSPs towards the sceptical conclusion that if all MSPs are equal, some are treated more equally than others.

Discontent on this issues and the realisation that the Parliament was poorly prepared to respond to them influenced the establishment of an Ad Hoc Liaison Group in July 1999, chaired by the Parliament's Deputy Presiding Officer George Reid MSP. It has published four core principles underpinning the new pattern of representation ushered in by devolution:

- A universal multi-member system in the Scottish Parliament, where every constituent and every part of Scotland is represented by eight MSPs.

- Equal status of MSPs, whether representing a constituency or a region, in relation to their parliamentary duties and activities.

- No 'poaching' - no constituency MSP should deal with, or seek to be involved in, a matter primarily relating to a constituent or issue outside his or her constituency and no regional MSP should deal with a matter primarily relating to a constituent or issue outwith his or her region.

- The interests of the particular constituent/locality should be paramount, as the determining factor in the allocation of representational duties.

The purpose of the Liaison Group was to devise some basic ground-rules for the practical operation of the representational functions of MSP roles and to offer guidance to the Parliament for each 'player' in the triangular relationship involving parliamentarians, constituents and agencies/organisations.

A consistent feature of our interviews with MSPs was the belief that members of the public have never been clear about who to approach with cases relating to the different tiers of government. If that was true when electors were represented by, at most, four politicians (District Councillor, Regional Councillor, MP and MEP until 1995), it will certainly be true in the new era when each Scottish elector may turn to eighteen elected representatives (one councillor, one constituency MSP, seven list MSPs, one MP and eight MEPs).

These principles offered a degree of clarity amid confusion in the early months of devolution. However, a number of the thorniest issues are not fully resolved by adherence to these guidelines, notably the perception that poaching and cherry-picking is occurring within regional constituencies by list members. The Scottish Affairs Select Committee report of 1998 on The Operation of Multi-Tier Democracy had anticipated as much:

> *MSPs will reach the Parliament by different routes ... We foresee this leading to difficulties as either they find themselves with different status doing different kinds of work, or they tread on each other's toes as voters play one off against the other. Problems may be particularly acute if the constituency and regional MSPs represent different parties.*
> **(House of Commons Scottish Affairs Select Committee, 1998: xxi)**

## WHAT DO MSPS SAY?

The panel of MSPs was asked about their early experiences. One participant had the early experience of attending a dinner where the speaker had addressed the guests as 'My Lords, Ladies, Gentlemen, MPs, MSPs and List MSPs'. Did others think the two types of member differed in responsibility and approach to the task of representation?

One SNP list member did not believe the public would distinguish between who is a constituency member and who is a regional list member: 'They only want someone to help them, so they go to the one who is most accessible'. The key element in the new pattern of representation is the greater choice it gives to the public:

> *Lazy constituency MSPs, who don't hold surgeries or play any part in the Parliament, will be easily exposed by list MSPs and vice*

*versa. The public will quickly recognise when (the constituency member) is doing nothing, and can now come to me for help, whereas before they would have had no alternative.*

One of Labour's constituency members argued that the two types of MSP are elected in 'equally legitimate but different ways'. She raised the question about the quality of accountability arising from the two different routes to the Parliament. She observed that if she did something her constituents strongly opposed, they could vote against her at the next election, but with list MSPs the only course of action available to electors is to stop voting for the party.

How do established parliamentarians - the dual mandate members - respond to the new breed of regional list members? One of the SNP's MP/MSPs argued that list members should develop specialist skills and become closely involved with the committee systems, on the assumption that MSPs will tend to refer reserved matters directly to their Westminster counterpart (while a significant part of the dual mandate member's time is spent on reserved matters). This MSP was the most enthusiastic of constituency members interviewed about the role of list members:

*List MSPs should not be regarded as second-class citizens. They have a huge role to play and, depending on the work they do and the image they project, will affect our whole attitude to the concept of PR. If they disappear into the background, they may set back the whole PR project.*

# TAKING THE INITIATIVE: SERVING CONSTITUENTS AND PICKING CHERRIES

One of the consistent themes raised in the initial interviews without prompting was the differing ability of MSPs to decide which issues they would focus their efforts on. Using the language of the Reid Liaison Group, MSPs vary in their role as initiators, and this is at least in part related to differences between constituency and list members. One of the SNP's dual mandate members argued that constituency members did not have to work as hard to generate casework or get noticed by the media or by organisations in the area:

*Constituency MSPs can sit back and let the problems come to you.*
*List MSPs must be more adventurous and self-starting. They will*
*have to work harder to establish the fact that they are there.*

On the other hand, one Labour constituency member expressed a view that has been heard more frequently since the Parliament began to establish itself. She believed that constituency MSPs had no choice but to deal with all the casework that comes their way. They are more likely to be the 'first port of call' for the majority of constituents, while list members have more freedom to pursue higher-profile and media-friendly issues and improve their profile. She described this as 'ambulance chasing'. Some of her colleagues have identified cases of so-called 'cherry picking' in their constituencies:

*I wouldn't like to think that list MSPs can pick and choose. The*
*responsibility goes with the job. If you're going to do it, you do it*
*across the board and all the time. You can't cherry pick issues for*
*political reasons rather than for public service reasons. There's no*
*doubt that this has happened.*

Moreover, it appears to matter what kind of 'cherry-picking' is going on. If a list member decides to specialise in a particular policy area with general regional significance (business support or legal reforms for example), this may be less threatening to constituency members than issues with more locally-specific implications. This MSP also believed more consideration should be given to definitions of geographical representation:

*Being a constituency MSP, my boundaries are very clear. The list*
*members are only entitled to represent issues for the (regional seat) as*
*a whole, they cannot sub-divide and package it up to suit themselves.*
*That's what they have done. It exposes them to the realities of politics,*
*but actually it is not legitimate within the terms of the political system.*

Politicians are likely to feel nervous when opponents of another party open an office in their constituency, especially when one party has represented the area for a long time. One dual mandate member explained: 'Constituency MSPs are proprietorial regarding their local area. They get frightened that the role of the list member will undermine them'.

In much of urban Scotland, Labour is experiencing this new and uncomfortable change as SNP members, Conservatives and others establish a competing power base in its traditional heartland. This raises questions about who 'owns' the right to represent constituents' interests, who 'won' and who 'lost' the election, and who has the best claim to speak for an area. Suddenly the rules of the game have changed. One Scottish Labour MSP summed up the new situation effectively: 'the opposition is no longer out of action as it is under the first past the post system'.

Many MSPs highlighted the practice of list members targeting a specific constituency (i.e. their own) with a view to winning in the first past the post section at the next election. In more than one region, the SNP's list members had taken an early decision to divide the constituency seats between them. In one of the safest Labour seats in the region, the SNP's constituency candidate from 1999 (and now a list member) is almost exclusively working in the same seat, seeking to perform all the same functions as the constituency member. While his Labour colleagues have been irritated by what they see as encroachment onto their territory, he believes it is rational for opposition politicians to maximise their position in this way:

*If we'd been in the same position, we'd have done the same. There is nothing you can do about it. Under FPTP the opposition disappears for five years. This is not the case now - there are MSPs everywhere. It is inevitable under PR. Some people who are normally in favour of PR are showing signs of resentment, because it challenges their hegemony. But at the end of the day, it makes the constituency MSP work harder; you have to be on your toes. In that sense it is better for the people.*

Constituency members appear to have mixed views about list members working 'on their patch'. One of the SNP's dual mandate members agreed that some list members were setting themselves up working in particular constituencies rather than across the whole region. As far as that puts pressure on the constituency MSP, he thought this was no bad thing: 'I could do without it, but for keeping people on their toes it is probably a good thing'.

Although there are clear concerns about the high profile achieved by some list members, other MSPs admitted that they would be quite happy for their list opponents to be involved in local casework 'because it would keep them

rethinking representation: some evidence from the first year occupied within the constituencies, leaving them less time for politics and keeping them out of trouble' (and presumably out of the news). As one Labour MSP representing a safe urban constituency observed:

*No one knows what list MSPs do. It is for all of us to try and set some sort of a pattern for what we expect. List members can hold surgeries in my constituency if they want and if they can solve issues that I can't then so be it.*

In public however, many Labour MSPs are unhappy that list members are working in their area, and particularly so over representational work with organisations than constituents. A number of examples have been reported in the Scottish press in recent months. In Ayrshire, the Health Board arranged a meeting to discuss proposed changes in health service funding. The Labour constituency MSPs and MPs protested when it emerged that regional list members were also invited to the meeting. Writing in a local newspaper, they stated that opposition list members had 'no mandate from the people' and would introduce conflicts of interest (reflecting the fact that list MSPs may represent regions taking in two or more Health Board or LEC areas). In turn this earned a rebuke from the Scottish Parliament's Presiding Officer.

It is difficult to see how 'cherry-picking' of issues (by area of interest) or by locality (by dividing up the regional constituency into smaller patches) breaches any of the Reid principles. As long as list members are not actively soliciting casework that a constituency member has already started to deal with, and are not 'passing the buck' on the everyday cases that have come their way, no rules have been broken. This pattern of representation is implicit in the different 'constituencies' the MSPs represent. In practice, the distinction may be reduced over time as constituency members seek to generate Scottish-wide media attention for various local cases, and as the committees provide a forum for further blurring the boundaries.

## CONCLUSION

In future waves of the MSP panel, the study will explore how constituency and list members are working out such difficulties in practice, and consider to what extent protocol based on experience as compared to a formal set of guidelines issued through the Parliament will provide a guide to future behaviour. In addition, we shall consider how MSPs deal with reserved matters within the remit of Westminster that are first referred to them by constituents:

- Do they pass the case on to the relevant Scottish MP at Westminster?

- In the case of regional members, is the 'relevant' MP someone from the same party or someone with particular expertise to respond to a constituent's concern?

- Are list members keener than FPTP constituency members to try to solve a social security matter for example, and are there any signs that MSPs from the governing coalition parties are prepared to do the same?

- How are Scottish MPs at Westminster adjusting to what should be a lighter mailbag - and do they refer devolved casework back to the relevant MSP?

This brief discussion based on preliminary findings from the first stage of the study indicates a degree of confusion around the appropriate roles of constituency and list MSPs. Guidelines offer a foundation by which experience can be tested, but they are by no means fully comprehensive. Nor is it self-evident that they could or should be at this stage in the Parliament's life. As the task of rethinking representation unfolds, it is essential that we enhance our understanding of what it means in practice and how it is being experienced by politicians across the tiers of government and by members of the public.

rethinking representation: some evidence from the first year

# SECTION 2 the new parliamentary structures

# CHAPTER 6: how the parliament works

## alice brown

This chapter addresses questions of how the Scottish Parliament works in practice and whether it has lived up to the plans designed by some of its architects. The demands for a Parliament in Scotland and the campaigns for constitutional change over the 1980s and 1990s were always closely connected to a vision of how the new institution would operate. A key aspect of the vision was that the Parliament should be 'different' from the Westminster model and its associated electoral and political systems. As the Scottish Constitutional Convention stated in 1995:

> *we have emerged with the powerful hope that the coming of a Scottish Parliament will usher in a way of politics that is radically different from the rituals of Westminster: more participative, more creative, less needlessly confrontational ... [with] ... a culture of openness which will enable the people of Scotland to see how decisions are being taken in their name, and why. The Parliament we propose is much more than a mere institutional adjustment. It is a means, not an end.*
>
> **(Scottish Constitution Convention, 1995: 9)**

Many of these themes were similarly echoed in the White Paper on devolution published by the newly elected Labour Government in 1997 (Scottish Office, 1997).

## ENVISIONING THE PARLIAMENT

The cross-party Consultative Steering Group (CSG) then considered the operational needs and working methods of the Parliament and developed proposals for the rules of procedure and standing orders. Backed by widespread public consultation, expert advice and research into the workings of other

Parliaments in Europe and elsewhere, the CSG published its report in January 1999 making the case for the Parliament's procedures to be based on the four key principles of Power-sharing, Accountability, Openness and Participation and Equal Opportunities (Consultative Steering Group, 1999: 3). The details of the procedures it recommended were founded on these principles.

Power-sharing involved appointing an independent Presiding Officer and an all-party Business Committee, as well as establishing all-purpose parliamentary committees with power to initiate, scrutinise and investigate legislation, and with a central role in the legislative process. Membership of committees was to reflect the political composition of the Parliament itself, so that no single party could dominate proceedings. Civic organisations were also to be involved in the policy process and arrangements were made for Public Petitions. To ensure greater accountability the CSG recommended a Code of Conduct for MSPs, a Standards Committee, as well as mechanisms such as parliamentary questions, and giving committees the power to conduct enquiries and take evidence from Ministers and civil servants. Powerful Finance and Audit Committees were also proposed.

Greater access and participation were to be achieved through an open, simple and modern style of operating, and parliamentary times which coincide with normal working hours and with Scottish school holidays. Plenary and committee meetings were normally to be held in public, with translation facilities for Gaelic and the publication of short reports and bulletins in several languages. To encourage wider participation, the legislative process was to allow maximum time for consultation and committees were to meet regularly outside Edinburgh; consideration was also to be given to basing some committees outside the capital. New ways of public consultation and participation, and new initiatives in education for citizenship were proposed, aided by information technology. To meet the equal opportunities objective, there was to be an Equality Unit in the Scottish administration and an Equal Opportunities Committee in the Parliament. The mainstreaming of equal opportunities throughout the work of the Parliament and the policies of the government was also recommended.

Transitional standing orders and procedures governed the first meetings of the Parliament after it began its work on May 12th 1999. Its first business was to elect the Presiding Officer and two Deputies before the election of the First Minister. The use of electronic voting caused some hilarity in the early days as some MSPs struggled to come to terms with the technology. The Parliament then acknowledged and endorsed the CSG's principles for procedures. In theory, therefore, the Parliament had the potential to operate and work in ways which could make it substantially different from the Westminster model - aside from the fact that it is elected on a more proportional electoral system which involves a different political balance between the parties.

However, new institutions and new procedures do not in themselves guarantee new ways of conducting politics and the creation of a different political culture. The theory of new parliamentary arrangements needs to become practice.

# THE PARLIAMENT IN OPERATION

The Parliament is elected on a fixed term of four years, making it impossible for the First Minister to select the date of the next or subsequent elections. The aim of observing more 'family friendly' hours has been achieved with the normal week beginning on Monday afternoon and finishing at lunch-time on Friday. A key weekly focus is First Minister's Question Time on Thursdays, although this was an aspect that had not been recommended by the CSG on the grounds that it might encourage some of the more negative aspects associated with Prime Minister's Question Time at Westminster.

In contrast to the euphoria that surrounded the opening of the Parliament on the July 1st 1999, the workings of the Parliament were soon subject to hostile media attention. The first controversy arose over the dispute about MSPs allowances and the distinction drawn between allowances paid to constituency and list MSPs. While this may seem a technicality, given the distribution of seats particularly between Labour and the SNP, there were key aspects of party politics at play. Relatedly, there was the dispute over 'Short money' or the money made available to the official opposition to carry out its business. While the concept of opposition has a somewhat different meaning in a Scottish Parliament with a coalition government operating under a system which gives six parties representation, again this disagreement very much reflected the party competition between Labour and the SNP. Party rivalries were also played out in the ongoing saga about the siting of the new Parliament building and the controversy over its escalating costs. In hindsight all of these matters could have been better dealt with in ways that did not open the Executive and the Parliament itself to public cynicism. They could have been handled, if not by the CSG, at least in the spirit of the CSG through involvement and negotiation between the main interests involved. Instead, the Parliament and the new politicians were portrayed to the public by the media - unfairly - as only being concerned with their own remuneration and in spending excessive amounts of money on a new building and facilities.

Early months also witnessed the beginnings of a struggle between an Executive seeking to get its business through and parliamentary committees with a remit to scrutinise the Executive. Other areas of controversy that received media attention included the so-called Scottish 'Lobbygate' affair, the rapid departure of certain Special Advisers and some of the private member's bills. The first big test for coalition politics and power-sharing centred on the unlikely topic of higher education and the difference of policy over student tuition fees. While all of these issues were not the responsibility of the Parliament per se, nevertheless they contributed to public perceptions of the working of the Parliament and the new MSPs.

More practical issues arose in implementing aspects of the CSG's recommendations, such as the time available for parliamentary business, the design of Question Time, the large number of written parliamentary questions being laid down and the time taken to receive answers, the time at which parliamentary voting takes place, the procedures for summing up in non-Executive debates, the amount of time allocated for non-Executive party business, and the selection procedures for deputy committee convenors. But again, while these may appear to be technical matters, they also have a political dimension. After all the design of parliamentary arrangements and procedures was intended to introduce ways of working in the Parliament that were different from Westminster where, for example, the Executive controls the timetabling of business which in turn impacts on the balance of power between the Executive and the Parliament.

## POLITICS AND PARTICIPATION IN THE PARLIAMENT

The Parliament and its workings have not been devoid of political controversy. In some respects, this may be rather unsurprising given the general cynicism that surrounds the operation of politics and the behaviour of politicians. But there are a number of ways to judge the first year of the workings of the Parliament: the role of the new political actors, the style and conduct of parliamentary business, access to the process of government, the level of information available to the public, detailed aspects of the procedures themselves, and the principles set out by the CSG.

The intention was that all MSPs should be actively engaged in the business of the Parliament whether or not they were Ministers. While some are clearly more active than others, the workload for the new politicians is potentially high as all in non-ministerial positions are involved in two parliamentary committees. Further, in spite of the 'family friendly' hours of the meetings of the Parliament and its committees, the work of the MSPs does not end at the close of parliamentary sessions. MSPs are also subject to a strict Code of Conduct that in some respects is more testing than their Westminster counterparts with failure to register certain interests subject to a criminal offence.

The style of operation in the Parliament is different in that it is much less formal and the procedures are more open and straightforward. But there are also aspects of continuity with Westminster such as the operation of the party whips, where backbench MSPs often feel excluded from the decisions of their own Executive. Further, perhaps predictably, the behaviour and conduct of MSPs in the chamber cannot always be described as non-confrontational and non-adversarial. There are also differences in the attitudes of MSPs between those more willing to endorse new styles of working and inclusive politics and others who have a more restricted view of representative democracy.

If one of the aims was to provide more participation in politics then access to the process of government in Scotland is provided through different routes and channels, for example through the committee structure or the Civic Forum which Lucy McTernan more fully discusses in her contribution (see Chapter Seventeen). There is no doubt that groups and organisations can have access to politicians in a way that is unprecedented. A surprisingly high number of people watch the Parliament from the public gallery. Facilities are used regularly by schools and colleges, and encouraged through the work of the Youth Parliament and the Education Officer.

Nevertheless, the extent to which participation has moved beyond the 'usual suspects' is limited, although the Parliament is endeavouring to extend the scope of participation through better public information and its web site, aided by the work of SPICE (Scottish Parliament Information Centre) and the Visitor Information Centre. But involving people who previously have had little interest in the parliamentary process is not something that can be achieved easily or quickly.

## THE EVOLVING PARLIAMENT

In terms of the detailed procedures themselves then, there have been some changes made to the recommendations of the CSG. It was intended that procedures would be adapted in practice to meet the needs of the Parliament, although it was hoped that in making procedural changes and deciding on the best methods of working the Parliament should hold to the four principles set out by the Steering Group. The process is described by one MSP in the following terms:

*In the UK Parliament if you come up against an obstacle there's a no entry sign and you have to turn round and go back. In the Scottish Parliament if you come up against an obstacle the discussion goes something like 'do we go over it, round it or under it?' The procedures of the Parliament can be moulded and are being moulded to suit the most effective way it can operate. That to me is the classic example of a modern, flexible, responsive Parliament that finds its own best way of operating.* **(1)**

It is important to emphasise just how different many of the aspects of procedure are from the Westminster model, such as the elections of the Presiding Officer and First Minister, its hours and ways of working, and its relationship with parliamentary committees, the Scottish Executive and with Scottish civic society. But some of these aspects may not be immediately apparent or important to members of the public who are more concerned with what the Parliament actually achieves in terms of its impact on health, education, employment and housing policy.

For some the Scottish Parliament may on the surface appear to be just a smaller version of Westminster, but those familiar with parliamentary systems know how different it is in some respects. Writing to his constituents and comparing the Scottish and Westminster Parliament, one MSP and MP stated that:

*None of this would have happened at Westminster. Nor would we have had debates about every Scottish issue under the sun as we have had over the past few months. I recently counted 25 speeches I have made in the plenary Scottish Parliament debates which is more than all the Scottish speeches I was able to make on the floor of the House of Commons in seven years, including my time as a Minister.* **(Chisholm, 2000)**

## CONCLUSION

After just one year of operation it is too early to draw any firm conclusions about the workings of the Scottish Parliament. The new institution is in its infancy and its members are still learning and experimenting in their new roles. The Parliament began by endorsing and operating on the principles outlined by the

CSG but there is some way to go before they will be fully realised. With regard to power-sharing, it has been something of a new experience for the Scottish Labour Party to learn to share power in the context of Scottish politics. Although they did not achieve an overall majority in the Parliament, they are the major and dominant partners in the coalition. Nevertheless, the acceptance of the main recommendations of the Cubie Committee (Independent Committee of Inquiry into Student Funding, 1999), which effectively led to the abolition of tuition fees, was one illustration of the new working of the Parliament in relation to the Executive and of coalition politics in action. The extent of power-sharing between the Parliament and the Executive, the Parliament and the civil service, and the Parliament and the people has yet to be fully tested. Again, one victory for the power of the legislators and the people over the Executive was claimed following the success of Tommy Sheridan's private member's bill on the abolition of warrant sales.

In terms of accountability there are new mechanisms in place as recommended by the CSG and the MSPs have to work to a strict Code of Conduct. In spite of the adverse publicity over 'Lobbygate', the Parliament and its procedures survived the experience and gained respect in the way in which the affair was handled. The workings of the Parliament are also much more visible and transparent than public affairs have been handled in the past in Scotland. The parliamentary committees have in addition played an important role in taking evidence from ministers, civil servants and from representatives of other public bodies.

Access and participation have been an important aspect of the ethos of the new Parliament and measures have been taken to encourage the involvement of individuals, groups and organisations. And there are initiatives to develop wider involvement and interest in politics. Such developments may not be as popular with some parliamentarians who hold more strongly to the traditions of representative democracy, and the challenge to bring new voices into the democratic process has still to be met.

Last but not least, there is the issue of equal opportunities. While positive developments were recorded in the setting up of an Equal Opportunities Committee in the Parliament and an Equality Unit in the Scottish Executive, concern was raised when it was mooted that the EO Committee might disappear with a re-organisation of the committee structure and incorporated into the work of another committee. This suggestion, however, was greeted with strong opposition. Work has begun to address aspects of the public appointments system in Scotland and the inclusion of members of communities who are traditionally excluded from key decision-making arenas. Again, there is a long way to go before all aspects of discrimination have been addressed.

We can conclude that there is a mixed picture to report. If comparison is made with Westminster then we can identify aspects of both continuity and change in terms of parliamentary procedures and public perceptions of the working of the Scottish Parliament and the role of MSPs. Many of the procedural aspects are considerably different from those operating at Westminster and the potential for the Parliament to be different in other respects is there. However, for many people in Scotland - especially those reliant on media coverage of the new institution - it may seem that the Parliament and its members fit preconceived stereotypes. Further, in terms of the principles outlined by the CSG, there have been both positive and negative developments.

As the Parliament grows and matures, much will depend on the balance of forces between MSPs and Ministers and the relationships with different levels of governance - local, Westminster and European. It will also depend on the relationships with others both within and outwith the formal parliamentary and governmental process, and the interaction between representative and participative democracy. Much hinges on how tensions are resolved between the interests of politicians keen to make their mark and to gain or retain power, the desire for technical efficiency on the part of those charged with the operation of the Parliament, and the values and aspirations of those political activists who are not in the Parliament.

In time it will be possible to judge more accurately whether, in its working, the Parliament has been successful in moving away from a model based on adversarial, zero-sum politics associated with Westminster to develop a more plural and inclusive form of politics based on alliances around key political objectives. Such processes are not unconnected to the policy outcomes on which the Scottish people will ultimately judge the Scottish Executive and the Scottish Parliament.

# ENDNOTE

(1) This quotation is drawn from research supported by the Economic and Social Research Council (Grant No.L32723009). The financial assistance obtained in carrying out this project is gratefully acknowledged.

how the parliament works

# CHAPTER 7: the first laws of the new parliament

## peter jones

The first legislative programme of the new Scottish Parliament was, as Donald Dewar, the First Minister, said when he announced it on June 16th 1999, another milestone in the passage of power from Westminster to Holyrood, as the new legislature was fast becoming known in shorthand. 'People ask: when will this Parliament begin to make a difference? Today, we begin to answer that question', (Scottish Parliament, June 16th 1999, col. 403) Mr Dewar said.

The first of the answers provided was in the size of the programme - eight bills. Under the Westminster regime, the most that any Scottish Secretary could hope for under an average parliamentary programme of 20 bills in a year was two bills. Sometimes, Scottish legislation could be tacked on to a primarily English and Welsh bill; sometimes, separate bits of legislation could be levered together in one bill as had occasionally happened with law reform; but, these stratagems apart, two bills was the maximum.

So this programme illustrated one of the reasons behind the demand for devolution - that a Scottish Parliament would have the time to devote to Scottish legislation which Westminster did not have. When the programme was announced, no-one had any idea whether eight bills was too many or too few for the Parliament to handle. Each bill would have to go through entirely new procedures of consultation and committee debate, some would have to be steered through by Ministers who had never done any such thing in their lives, and be discussed by politicians who were complete novices to the business of legislating. Only by trying it out could it be found out whether the Parliament could cope. And, as Dewar noted: 'There is much to be done' (ibid, col. 405).

# THE FIRST LEGISLATIVE PROGRAMME OF THE SCOTTISH EXECUTIVE

The bills that were announced by Dewar on June 16th 1999 were:

## Land Reform
This was very much the Executive's flagship bill. It was intended to give communities the right to buy the land on which they lived and worked when that land was put up for sale by the owner. Abuses by a few landowners, particularly in the Highlands by owners living away from their estates, had made reform a political priority. The bill would also create a right of responsible access for walkers and climbers.

## Abolition of Feudal Tenure
Again, a few well-publicised abuses of the peculiarly Scottish and medieval system of land tenure had made its abolition a pressing political concern. Feudal superiors - people who do not own land, but who own rights to approve or disapprove of what happens on land and to charge for the privilege - would lose those rights.

## National Parks
Long debate in Scotland had veered towards accepting the argument that there were areas of the country of such outstanding beauty and under such pressure from visitors that they now required the kind of protection and management which had long been available through the National Parks system in England and Wales.

## Ethical Standards in Local Government
Though Mr Dewar of course did not spell this out, public concern about the behaviour of councillors in certain councils, all Labour-controlled and to which the media had devoted a vast amount of attention, had risen to the point where doing something had become imperative. This bill would establish a Scottish Standards Commission to scrutinise councillors' behaviour against a new Code of Conduct.

## Incapable Adults
This was very much an area - how people who have become, through mental or other incapacity, unable to look after their own affairs - where the law had become outdated and needed drastic modernisation.

### Transport
This was intended to create the legal framework through which it would become possible to introduce tolls on motorways, charge motorists driving into congested city centres, allow councils to levy charges on workplace parking and to update the regulations covering bus routes and operators.

### Financial Procedures and Auditing
Any Parliament to which an Executive is accountable needs a set of rules under which that Executive spends taxpayers' money and is held to account by the Parliament. This bill would not authorise public spending, but would create the rules for doing so.

### Education
According to Mr Dewar, this was also a flagship bill. It would put duties on local authorities to raise standards and tackle the problems of underperforming schools, set out a national framework for local control of schools, enable the Executive to expand pre-school provision, and allow the Executive to take back into local authority control those few Scottish schools which had opted to become self-governing.

Very little in this programme required negotiation between Labour and the Liberal Democrats. All were contained, to a greater or lesser extent, in the two parties' manifestos. By usual political standards, it was a relatively uncontroversial programme. The most contentious item, singled out for attack by both Alex Salmond, the SNP leader, and David McLetchie, the Conservative leader, was the Transport Bill, particularly its motorway tolling provisions. Indeed, such was the political onslaught on this item in the ensuing months, that the Executive soon put this aspect on the back burner.

The media thought it unexciting too. Partly this was because much of it had been well trailed beforehand and therefore was not new to reporters. Some commentators had expected a Housing Bill, but since consultation on a housing White Paper had concluded just days beforehand, this expectation was unrealistic. A Freedom of Information Bill, dear to the heart of Jim Wallace, the Minister for Justice, was not included either, simply because the process of consultation meant that it could not commence legislative scrutiny until the second year.

But the programme lacked a populist edge. Including a bill to abolish the warrant sale method of debt recovery would have filled that part and would have avoided the embarrassing mess the Executive got into in April 2000 when trying to deal with a private member's bill on warrant sales. The virtue of dullness, however, lay in providing a programme on which the new Parliament and new politicians could cut their teeth without getting into too much party political controversy.

Controversy, however, soon flared when Wendy Alexander, the Minister for Communities, announced that the local government Ethical Standards Bill would also abolish legislation by the previous Conservative Government prohibiting local authorities and schools from 'promoting' homosexuality. The row over Clause 2A, or Section 28, as it became variously known, split the Executive over the desirability of replacing, rather than just repealing, a discriminatory law with laws over what pupils should and should not be taught in sex education. Press reporting of this row and the financing of a private referendum on the issue by Brian Souter, the rich chairman of Stagecoach, almost completely obscured the rest of the legislative programme.

## 'EVENTS, DEAR BOY!'

While an Executive can plan a programme, it also has to deal with events. On August 2nd 1999, at Lanark Sheriff Court, Sheriff John Douglas Adam ruled that Noel Ruddle, a psychopathic killer who had been sent to Carstairs State Hospital in 1992 for using a Kalashnikov rifle to kill a neighbour, should be set free. He was apparently suffering from a personality disorder which was said to be untreatable, and which was not the original condition for which he was sent to Carstairs.

Public and ministerial reaction was one of incredulity and outrage. Several more such killers were thought to be preparing to use this escape route. And, if the particular circumstances of the Ruddle case applied to them, the law said they should be freed. So the law had to be changed to allow sheriffs to take public safety into consideration when dealing with such cases and to widen the definition of mental disorder to include personality disorder.

Thus, while MSPs might have wished for another, and more noble, milestone, the Mental Health (Public Safety and Appeals) (Scotland) Bill became the first piece of legislation to be passed by the Parliament. Using emergency procedures, it was rushed through on September 8th 1999 by the whole Parliament sitting as a committee, and swiftly received Royal Assent later that month on September 13th. Because of the need to change questions in the decennial population census being held in 2000, the emergency procedures were also used to rush through another short bill - the Census (Amendment) (Scotland) Bill - which allows details of people's religion to be collected.

Apart from the need to incorporate unforeseen legislative elements, it also became apparent that private members bills would occupy much legislative time, perhaps more so than had been envisaged by the legislative process designers. Two bills received much publicity. Mike Watson, Labour MSP for Glasgow Cathcart, introduced the Protection of Wild Mammals (Scotland) Bill, intended to ban fox and other hunting with dogpacks. Tommy Sheridan, Scottish Socialist MSP for Glasgow, introduced the Abolition of Poindings and Warrant Sales Bill.

The latter bill caused the Executive an embarrassing defeat. All along, the bill was felt to have a flaw in failing to create an adequate alternative for recovering debt from poor people. This, Ministers argued, would mean that the poor would lose access to credit and loans and could ignore council tax bills with impunity. At Westminster, the government can use any of a dozen devices to kill off a bill that it does not like. The Scottish Executive however, has no such freedom. As Sheridan's bill progressed through three parliamentary committees, a large number of Labour MSPs became convinced that its merits outweighed its flaws. So, in a vote by the whole Parliament on April 27th 2000 to move it on to the next stage, an Executive attempt to stop the bill failed because of a Labour rebellion. This rebellion was a clear indication that the Executive does not have anything like the total control of the legislative process that the government has at Westminster and the first exertion by the Parliament of its right to control its part of the legislative process.

The point is underlined when looking at the state of legislative progress on May 5th 2000. Six Executive bills have been passed: the Census Amendment Bill, the Ruddle case bill, the Financial Procedures Bill, a bill for the 2000/2001 budget, the Adults with Incapacity Bill and the bill abolishing feudal tenure. Seven bills were in progress, but only three were from the Executive - the bills for ethical standards, national parks and education. Four were private members' bills - the two already discussed, plus a minor bill by Tavish Scott, the Shetland Liberal Democrat MSP, to amend shellfishing regulations, and a bigger one by Robert Brown, a Glasgow Liberal Democrat MSP, to change the law on homelessness and housing tenure.

It is almost certain that at least two of the eight bills originating from the Executive will not get passed in the first year. Consultation on the Land Reform

Bill threw up the need to expand it to include changes to crofting law, thereby delaying its progress. Controversy over congestion charges will also prolong discussion of the Transport Bill when it is introduced.

Two other bills were also signalled during the first year. One was a bill to make aspects of the Scottish judicial system comply with the European Convention on Human Rights (ECHR). The need for this arose when the Court of Session ruled that the use of temporary sheriffs in the courts, though a long-established practice, was against the ECHR which had been made justiciable in the Scottish courts thanks to the legislation establishing the Parliament.

The other bill was necessitated by the need for a bill to regulate the use of investigatory powers, such as covert surveillance and the interception of communications, by Scottish police forces. This bill was necessitated by parallel legislation for the rest of the UK introduced at Westminster.

Just as interesting as the areas or subjects on which Holyrood has chosen to legislate are the areas or subjects on which it has chosen not to legislate. It should not be forgotten that Westminster still has the right to legislate for Scotland, even in areas where legislative responsibility has been devolved to Holyrood. This has happened on three occasions up to May 1st 2000. Two have been uncontroversial - concerning rules for absent voting in the Representation of the People Bill, and charges levied under the Sea Fishing Grants (Charges) Bill. In both cases, motions allowing Westminster to legislate were passed without debate in the Parliament.

The third area is more interesting. Prior to the Scottish Parliament's inception, Westminster had begun debating the Sexual Offences (Amendment) Bill, the main purpose of which was to reduce the age of consent for homosexual activity from 18 to 16 years of age, so bringing it into line with the age of consent for heterosexual consent. Obstruction in the House of Lords meant that the bill fell at the end of the first Westminster parliamentary session. When it was reintroduced, responsibility for this matter had been devolved to the Scottish Parliament. But the Parliament voted to let Westminster do the work on behalf of Scotland. Rather surprisingly, and apparently paradoxically, the SNP voted for Westminster to carry on, while the Conservatives voted for Holyrood to debate the issue.

The reason is that the government intended to reintroduce the bill and use the Parliament Act to override any further Lords obstruction. But it could not do that

the first laws of the new parliament

if the bill was amended to remove the Scottish part of the legislation. The SNP were persuaded that this would delay a reform which they favoured, while the Tories were opposed to the age of consent change.

But it is also reasonable to point out that this tactic neatly avoided the Parliament being embroiled in another row comparable to the Clause 2A controversy. That would have absorbed even more ministerial, members', and civil service time and effort which appears to be severely over-stretched already.

This over-stretch showed on a number of occasions. Delays, caused by the time needed by the Executive to draft amendments, occurred during the committee stage of the Adults with Incapacity Bill. The Justice and Rural Affairs Committees also became overloaded with legislation to the extent that members complained they were unable to pursue their own lines of inquiry.

Generally, however, while the Executive has not made as much legislative progress as it wanted, the progress that has been made is remarkable. For a new Parliament, using new procedures, to get through the amount of business that it has in eight months of work in the first year (and which would have taken four years at Westminster) is a pretty good start by any standards.

# economic development

## tracey white

On publishing its first report of 2000 - the conclusions of the eight month long Inquiry into the Delivery of Local Economic Development Services in Scotland - the Scottish Parliament Enterprise and Lifelong Learning Committee could not 'stress highly enough that the first crucial step to improving the effectiveness of services to consumers must be to bring an end to competition between publicly funded organisations' (John Swinney MSP, Committee Convenor, May 10th 2000).

This finding appears to have been largely based on evidence from the business community, of 'congestion, confusion and duplication in the provision of economic development services from local enterprise companies, local authorities and enterprise trusts'.

The case for rationalising the delivery of services to business may indeed have been well made. But identifying action to address problems in the way the current system operates in this regard as the 'crucial first step' seems to miss the point that business support services only constitute a subset of possible economic development policy interventions. It also fails to reflect the need to build an economy which meets the priorities and aspirations of all Scotland's people.

In ensuring that the plethora of organisations contributing to the development of Scotland's economy best serve Scotland, should not the crucial first step, and for that matter the on-going emphasis, be the delivery of accessibility, transparency and equality in the economic development policy process?

In practical terms that requires a commitment to give more weight to the views of local communities in preparing and implementing local development strategies. It requires that the local economic forums recommended by the committee seek a much broader constituency than the minimum membership of local authorities, LECs, chambers of commerce, area tourist boards, and local higher and further education institutions. The inclusion of local workforce representatives would not be a bad start.

# CHAPTER 8:   the committee system of the scottish parliament

## peter lynch

The committee system of the Scottish Parliament was one of the innovative aspects of the new devolution settlement. It was intended to merge the functions of the standing and select committees at Westminster and operate as the Scottish Parliament's revising chamber: to consider and revise government legislative proposals in the absence of a second chamber. Parliamentary committees were given six specific functions in the Consultative Steering Group's (1999: 5) report on the functioning of the Parliament:

- *to consider and report on the policy and administration of the Scottish administration;*
- *to conduct inquiries into such matters or issues as the Parliament may require;*
- *to scrutinise primary and secondary legislation and proposed European Union legislation;*
- *to initiate legislation;*
- *to scrutinise financial proposals and administration of the Scottish Executive;*
- *to scrutinise procedures relating to the Parliament and its Members.*

Following inter-party negotiations after the May 1999 election, the Parliament instituted a committee system that established eight mandatory committees and eight subject committees. The pattern of committees largely followed the Consultative Steering Group's blueprint, though some were influenced by the ministerial composition of the Scottish Executive such as Enterprise and Lifelong Learning, and Transport and Environment. The composition of committees was intended to reflect the balance of party strengths on the Mound. Therefore, committees reflected the cross-party nature of the chamber, with a Labour minority but coalition majority on each committee as well as the sharing out of committee convenors between the four parties to reflect the multi-party nature of the Parliament (see Table 5).

However, in addition to the 16 mandatory and subject committees, two other important committees exist. The Parliamentary Bureau operates as the Business Committee of the Parliament. It comprises the Presiding Officer and the business managers of the four main parties. It determines the business programme of the plenary sessions, through timetabling legislation, selecting motions for debate and allocating debating times to the government and opposition. The second important committee is the Convenor's Liaison Committee. This committee developed as a management mechanism for the convenors of the 16 committees to discuss committee business.

## Table 5: The Committee System of the Scottish Parliament

| Subject Committees | Convenor | Members |
|---|---|---|
| Justice and Home Affairs | SNP | 11 |
| Education, Culture and Sport | Labour | 11 |
| Social Inclusion | Labour | 11 |
| Enterprise and Lifelong Learning | SNP | 11 |
| Health and Community Care | Liberal Democrat | 11 |
| Transport and the Environment | Labour | 11 |
| Rural Affairs | Conservative | 11 |
| Local Government | Labour | 11 |
| **Mandatory Committees** | | |
| Standards | LiberalDemocrat | 7 |
| Procedures | Conservative | 7 |
| Audit | SNP | 11 |
| Finance | Labour | 11 |
| European | Labour | 13 |
| Equal Opportunities | Labour | 13 |
| Public Petitions | Labour | 7 |
| Subordinate Legislation | SNP | 7 |

The committees were intended to be the centre-piece of the Parliament. Indeed, the Parliament meets as often in committee as it does in plenary session - one and half days for each. However, whilst the committees are where the Parliament's business is conducted in terms of detailed legislative scrutiny, questioning of Ministers, civil servants and investigation into specific policy areas and public organisations, the committee system remains an obscure institution to the public. The simple reason is that the media is more interested in set-piece debates in the Parliament chamber or the drama of First Minister's Question Time than the in-depth and rather dull committee meetings. Eleven MSPs sitting round a table discussing rural affairs or local government is not a particularly photogenic occasion. When the committees discuss detailed legislation and amendments they sink even further from the public eye.

However, such a negative view of the committees is certainly unfair. For, on occasions, they do gain a public profile through their work and gain media coverage. Minister for Justice, Jim Wallace, had two uncomfortable appearances before the Justice and Home Affairs Committee concerning the Noel Ruddle case and prison closures. Both appearances were covered by the evening news. Grilling of Ministers is perhaps the most likely committee activity to attract media attention, though not the sole one. The Public Petitions Committee gained coverage of its investigation into the Stobhill secure unit and its meeting in Galashiels to receive the Borders rail petition. Enterprise and Lifelong Learning hit the headlines with its economic development inquiry and the Transport and Environment Committee's report into telecommunications was widely reported across television, radio and the newspapers.

## COMMITTEE WORKLOADS AND INVESTIGATIONS

Committee workloads and activities have varied in the first year of the Parliament. Some of the variety is a consequence of the type of committee involved rather than the (in)activity of the MSPs who are members. However, it should be pointed out that each committee is unique. Each has a different remit, membership, level of activity and culture. For example, the Public Petitions Committee solely meets to discuss petitions and act upon them. It does not consider legislation or hold investigations, though it did examine the consultation process for the Stobhill secure unit following a petition. The Subordinate Legislation Committee only meets to discuss subordinate legislation: obscure orders and instruments that provoke little attention, but are necessary to renew and enforce many aspects of Scottish law. The Standards Committee found its first year dominated by the design of a Code of Conduct for MSPs as well as a number of individual inquiries such as 'Lobbygate', in which some Ministers were accused of providing access to lobbying firm Beattie Media. The Procedures Committee dealt with the Parliament's standing orders and business procedures - altering the procedures for First Minister's Question Time to make it a more dramatic event.

Other committees have had a more wide-ranging workload over 1999-2000, covering legislation, subordinate legislation, petitions and a number of their own inquiries. Some committees found their agendas largely determined by the legislative programme of the Scottish Executive. For example, the first year of the Justice and Home Affairs Committee was dominated by consideration of the Abolition of Feudal Tenure etc (Scotland) Bill, the Adults with Incapacity (Scotland) Bill and the Abolition of Poindings and Warrant Sales Bill. The committee launched a number of small inquiries but found its meetings dominated by its role as a revising chamber. By way of contrast, some committees had no government legislation to consider in the first year of the Parliament such as Enterprise and Lifelong Learning, though most committees had subordinate legislation to consider in addition to having some legislation referred to them by the Executive or other committees.

## Table 6: Meetings of Committees: June 1999 to the end of March 2000

| Committee | Number of Meetings | |
| --- | --- | --- |
| | 1999 | 2000 |
| Audit | 8 | 4 |
| Education, Culture and Sport | 11 | 11 |
| Enterprise and Lifelong Learning | 9 | 7 |
| Equal Opportunities | 9 | 9 |
| European Union | 10 | 7 |
| Finance | 10 | 8 |
| Health and Community Care | 16 | 8 |
| Justice and Home Affairs | 14 | 13 |
| Local Government | 12 | 11 |
| Procedures | 9 | 5 |
| Public Petitions | 6 | 6 |
| Rural Affairs | 11 | 8 |
| Social Inclusion | 12 | 13 |
| Standards | 16 | 6 |
| Subordinate Legislation | 14 | 11 |
| Transport and Environment | 8 | 6 |
| Total | 175 | 133 |

The number of meetings held by individual committees raises some questions about parliamentary activism. Some committees are clearly more entrepreneurial than others and determined to push ahead on a range of issues. However, even here the number of committee meetings is deceptive as so much committee work takes place behind the scenes. For example, the Equal Opportunities Committee has three sets of subcommittees and reporters that deal with race, gender and sexuality. The Local Government Committee's inquiry into local government reform involved a large number of visits to individual councils throughout Scotland. Most other committees had aspects of their work that involved meetings and visits outside the scheduled public meetings of the committee itself.

The manner in which committees instituted their own investigations was also highly varied. For example, a number of committees sought to deal with in-depth investigations over a 3-4 month period. Thus, rather than focus on small inquiries, Transport and Environment held a four month investigation into telecommunications planning (Transport and Environment Committee, 2000), Social Inclusion studied housing stock transfer from November 1999 to April 2000 and Enterprise and Lifelong Learning spent most of their first year on two inquiries into economic development agencies (Enterprise and Lifelong Learning Committee, 1999), and tourism. Other committees instituted briefer inquiries and reports into single issues. The wide-ranging remit of the Equal Opportunities Committee led it to conduct short inquiries into issues such as the MacPherson Report on the Stephen Lawrence case, the police complaints procedure, the impact of the European Convention on Human Rights and the situation of asylum seekers in Scotland. The Rural Affairs Committee held short inquiries that produced reports on the Scottish Adjacent Waters Boundaries Order and the Agricultural Business Improvement Scheme (Rural Affairs Committee, 1999a and 1999b).

The committee system was intended to be a power-sharing mechanism that operated by consensus. However, some committees are rather partisan in their style and operation, though this fact is often concealed within private sessions. Anyone attending the Education, Culture and Sport Committee could not but fail to be struck by the partisan nature of the committee meetings. The presence of two opposition party spokespersons on education - Brian Monteith (Conservative) and Nicola Sturgeon (SNP) - is part of the reason for this situation. Party points are made and debated, there is a good deal of argument between the members of the committee and votes have been held - something that has never occurred in some committees! And yet, despite partisan tensions, the Education, Culture and Sport Committee functioned effectively in all aspects of its work in its first year. Indeed, divisions within the committee did not prevent it from investigating broadcasting policy with questioning of staff from both the BBC and Grampian: even though broadcasting was a policy reserved to Westminster under Schedule 5 of the Scotland Act (1998).

# THE COMMITTEES AND DEMOCRATIC INVOLVEMENT

The Consultative Steering Group report did not merely outline the legislative and investigative functions of committees. It also gave them a prominent role in the new Scottish democracy in two ways. First, they were intended to operate as a second opposition, through acting as an independent revising chamber. Second, the committees were intended to ensure that the Parliament was open, responsive and accessible to the public through a number of measures such as travelling around Scotland, involving the public in its activities and using petitions as a means to facilitate public involvement in the Parliament's work. Both of these aspects of committee performance have been variable.

The independence of committees has not been easy to verify. On the one hand, it is obvious that each committee has a membership that provides a coalition majority, though when votes occurred Labour and Liberal Democrat MSPs did not always vote together. However, the government/opposition roll of committee members has had some bearing on their performance. They are, after all, party representatives rather than independent constituency members in the tradition of Edmund Burke. Despite this constraint, there have been occasions in which committees have opposed government. The Equal Opportunities Committee opposed the Scottish Executive on the Census Order and was prepared to force an amendment to the bill to ensure a question on religion: until the Executive relented. The Local Government Committee opposed many aspects of the Executive's proposals for local government reform: especially the notion of elected provosts. The Social Inclusion Committee effectively opposed the Executive's proposals for housing stock transfer, evident from its inquiry into the issue. Whether such opposition amends or overturns Executive legislation remains to be seen as there has not been enough contentious legislation so far in the Parliament. One indication might be the Executive's withdrawal of opposition to Tommy Sheridan's warrant sales abolition bill after support for it was garnered amongst Labour backbenchers working on the committees which had discussed the bill.

One obvious area in which the committees performance has been lacking has been in travelling around Scotland. The Consultative Steering Group (1999: 10) report stated that:

*the Parliament must be a Parliament for the whole of Scotland - not just for Edinburgh ... we realise that credence will only be given to this commitment if the Parliament actively involves other areas of Scotland. We propose that committees should be encouraged to meet and to take evidence outside Edinburgh, particularly when the subject matter might affect people staying in a particular area of Scotland, and that in a number of cases committees should have their permanent base somewhere other than Edinburgh.*

However, this agenda of geographical inclusion was largely ignored in the Parliament's first year. Parliamentary committees only met outside Edinburgh on one occasion out of 175 in 1999 - with Enterprise and Lifelong Learning meeting in Inverness. This situation improved slightly in 2000, with seven committee meetings out of 133 outside Edinburgh by the end of March 2000: two in Glasgow, three in Stirling, one in Galashiels and one in Brussels. However, not only is the geographical spread extremely limited - Glasgow and Stirling - but so is the involvement of committees. Two meetings each were held by the European and Local Government Committees, in addition to single meetings by Justice and Home Affairs, Public Petitions and Social Inclusion. Subject committees such as Education, Culture and Sport, Health and Community Care, Rural Affairs and Transport and Environment failed to venture outside of Edinburgh (Lynch, forthcoming 2000).

The subject committees of the Parliament also become the focus of pressure group attention. Groups such as the Scottish National Farmers Union now have a Rural Affairs Committee at which to direct their attentions. The largest teacher's union, the Educational Institute for Scotland (EIS), now has an Education, Culture and Sport Committee and the campaign group for the homeless, Shelter, has the Social Inclusion Committee. Consultation therefore largely involved the usual suspects rather than the general public - despite the intention of making the process more open to 'groups traditionally excluded from the decision-making process' (Consultative Steering Group, 1999: 7).

Indeed, ironically, it was the traditionally 'included' who gained access. The Business in the Chamber event organised by the Enterprise and Lifelong Learning Committee involved a consultation exercise with business organisations in the Parliament chamber. This was the sole example of this phenomenon and one that involved the traditional opponents of a Scottish Parliament. Furthermore, the development of 'clientelistic' relations between some subject committees and their main pressure groups associated with that policy area cannot be ruled out. This fact raises the potential for committees to go native and become supporters of particular interest groups. Arguably, this scenario may already have occurred with the Local Government Committee: a committee comprised of former councillors and local authority employees, which has echoed council concerns over local government reform and put its weight behind the recommendations of the McIntosh Commission on local government and the Scottish Parliament (Commission on Local Government, 1999). Acting as a lobbyist for COSLA was not exactly what the Consultative Steering Group had in mind for the Local Government Committee.

## CONCLUSION

The first year of operation of the Parliament's committee system was a highly differentiated experience due to the nature and functions of the committees themselves. However, several issues are worth noting. First, the committees and their members are clearly much further forward than in the early months of the Parliament. Their learning curve may have been steep, but it was a learning curve. The experience of committee work, investigations and detailed scrutiny of policy areas and legislation has radically improved the specialist skills of individual MSPs. Their ability to challenge the government and act as an effective revising chamber markedly improved as they got to grips with their subject areas and this situation will continue to improve across the life of the Parliament. Scrutiny of quangos rather than the Scottish Executive was the most visible manifestation of this development in the Parliament's first year: as committees heavily scrutinised Scotland's unelected government. Also, over time, links between the committees will improve committee working. Co-operation between committees, committee convenors and the experience of MSPs who serve on more than one committee will feed into increased committee effectiveness and possibly also assertiveness.

Second, the all-Scotland aspect to the committee system failed. Committees have largely been creatures of Edinburgh and therefore contributed to the perception of devolution leading to a new centralisation. The MSPs, Parliament and Executive did not cover themselves in glory in their first year of operation and the committees did little to assuage this situation by reaching out to the public and travelling across Scotland. Despite this problem, the committees did fulfil five of the six functions envisaged by the Consultative Steering Group report outlined above. The area in which they have been lacking has been in relation to proposing legislation. Significantly, no committee has proposed legislation, which contrasts with a growing number of MSPs' bills making their way through the Parliament's legislative process. However, a number of committees made their mark in amending Executive legislation and effectively holding Scottish government to account for its actions.

Of course, of late, some in the Parliament began to debate the effectiveness of the committee system in relation to the cost of the 16 committees (Hardie, 2000). Doubtless, they reflected on the differential workloads and performance of the committees outlined above, with suggestions that the Equal Opportunities, Petitions and Procedures Committees could become casualties of reform. Clearly, there is room for adjustment to the committee system. The system owes its design to the CSG blueprint of early 1999 and the post-election negotiations of May 1999. After a year of activity, it is not surprising that the committee structure could be revised. However, changes to the structure will prove both controversial and unpopular with the MSPs involved. The axing of committees, committee places and convenorships will be resisted by some MSPs and the revised scheme may not make the Parliament more effective. It may only increase the workload of the remaining committees.

# TAG THEATRE COMPANY CONGRESS OF NATIONS MANIFESTO

TAG Theatre Company has developed a three year programme of work related to government, democracy and the Parliament. The aim is to encourage the young people of Scotland to feel that it is their Parliament too. Launched in early 1999, the programme included Sense of Community, at the heart of which was a drama initiative through which school children could engage in an imaginative way with issues and questions about the real world by creating and running their own imagined communities.

At the three day Congress of Nations in December 1999, representatives from the participating schools travelled to Edinburgh to work together developing their drama-based imaginations and also to debate issues related to the real lives of young people today in Scotland. The Congress was held in the main chamber of the Scottish Parliament and was attended by a number of MSPs, including Sir David Steel, Patricia Ferguson, George Reid, Rhona Brankin and Nicola Sturgeon. The children debated the following motion:

*This Congress asks the Scottish Parliament to make the future of young people in Scotland its first priority and should concentrate on the following issues ...*

At the end of the debate, the children produced a manifesto based on that motion, and the following issues were chosen as the top twelve priorities for the young people attending the Congress.

## TOP FOUR PRIORITIES

- Health - Scotland has a very poor health record which we need to overcome.
- Sport and Leisure Facilities - better sports facilities improve health and keep children out of trouble.
- Education - all education should be free with no tuition fees, more specialist teachers, smaller classes and better education about drugs and alcohol.
- Homeless Young People - everyone should have a home.

# REMAINING PRIORITIES

- Safer Streets - including street lighting, more pedestrian crossings and more education about how to handle dangerous situations.
- Disabled People - more access for disabled people to all public spaces.
- Environment - if people destroy the environment it will destroy animals' homes.
- School Dinners - should be cheaper, with more variety and larger helpings.
- Work Experience - children should have more work experience and more chances to volunteer in areas or jobs which interest them.
- Youth Parliament - there should be a Youth Parliament to let children vote.
- Libraries - improve libraries with new books, a wider selection of authors and new computers.
- Road Safety - it is important to make roads safer for children by adding more zebra crossings, speed bumps and cycle tracks and by lowering the speed limit outside schools.

# CHAPTER 9: the first minister and the scottish executive

## robert pyper

During the period between the UK general election in May 1997 and the implementation of devolution in Scotland just over two years later, most public, media, and 'expert' attention was focused on the new Parliament rather than the post of First Minister and the Scottish Executive. There was a general assumption that Labour would emerge as the largest party in the Parliament, and, as a consequence there was some early interest in who would be the party's candidate for the post of First Minister. Once Donald Dewar had emerged as the clear favourite, attention switched back to the Parliament.

During the 'pre-devolution' period, it was not entirely clear that there was broad public understanding of the role and function of the First Minister, or of the relationship between the person who would occupy this post, the Scottish Executive Ministers and the Parliament. Similarly, the relationship between the ministerial team heading the new Scottish Executive and the former Scottish Office (now the Scotland Office) was not widely understood.

To some extent this lack of understanding could be attributed to the fact that the key founding documents for the Scottish devolution settlement, the White Paper, the report of the Consultative Steering Group in 1999, and the Scotland Act (1998), provided only a general framework for the operation of the new system of Scottish governance. The White Paper covered the Scottish Executive in two paragraphs and briefly mentioned ministers on two other occasions (Scottish Office, 1997). The Consultative Steering Group's final report devoted more space to the functions and role of the Parliament's Presiding Officer than to the Ministers and the Scottish Executive (Consultative Steering Group, 1999). The Scotland Act was scarcely more expansive, and concentrated on the constitutional formalities (Scotland Act, 1998). Initial academic analysis of the likely development of the First Minister's post and the Executive (see, for example, Leicester and McKay, 1998; Burrows, 1999) therefore had little to work on.

The relative vagueness was perhaps an advantage, inasmuch as it gave the new First Minister and the ministerial team the opportunity to set their own tone and establish their own pattern. Nonetheless, it is fair to say that both 'popular' and 'elite' expectations of these crucial elements of the devolution settlement were fairly vague. There was perhaps some, fairly generalised, feeling that the 'new politics' in Scotland (which would partly be engendered by the likelihood of coalition government), coupled with the arrival of fresh ministerial talent, would lead to a brand of executive governance which differed in key respects from that to be found at Westminster and Whitehall. In particular, there seemed to be a reasonable prospect of a more collegiate 'Cabinet' as opposed to 'Prime Ministerial' form of government. Beyond this prospect, it appeared that there was all to play for.

## CHARACTERISTICS AND STYLE OF THE NEW EXECUTIVE

The new government of Scotland which emerged following the Parliament's approval of Donald Dewar as First Minister on May 13th 1999 was a Cabinet of eleven, supported by a further eleven Deputy Ministers. It exhibited some striking features. For a start, it was that rare creature in British politics, a coalition. The Liberal Democrats took four ministerial posts overall, including two Cabinet positions (Jim Wallace became Deputy First Minister and Minister for Justice while Ross Finnie became Minister for Rural Affairs). Women were appointed to five posts, three of which were in the Cabinet. Wendy Alexander, Susan Deacon and Sarah Boyack were the youngest members of the Cabinet, which had a relatively low average age (by Westminster standards) of under 46.

The Executive appeared to offer a sound blend of experience and freshness, with the Whitehall ministerial veterans Donald Dewar, Henry McLeish and Sam Galbraith sitting alongside colleagues who were new to elective politics let alone ministerial life. Dewar's personal style was naturally collegiate, and this would set the tone for the conduct of Executive business.

Two key documents, produced in August 1999, set out the basic 'rules of the game' for the Executive's operation. The Scottish Ministerial Code (Scottish Executive, 1999c) was a tailored version of the UK code of conduct and guidance for Ministers. The Guide to Collective Decision Making (Executive Secretariat, 1999) developed themes which had been set out in the Scottish Ministerial Code and in the *Partnership for Scotland* (Scottish Executive, 1999b) agreement written by Dewar and Wallace as leaders of the Scottish Labour Party and the Scottish Liberal Democrats. The guide outlined in general terms the working relationship between the First Minister and the Deputy First Minister and explained the principles and procedures of collective decision making. The Cabinet would meet weekly (normally on Tuesday mornings) to perform its prime role as the body which 'reconciles Ministers' individual responsibilities with their collective responsibility and is the ultimate arbiter of all policy on devolved matters' (Executive Secretariat, 1999: para. 4.1).

The First Minister and the Executive were served by an Executive Secretariat, within which would be located the Cabinet Secretariat, an External Relations Division, a Constitutional Policy and Parliamentary Liaison Division and a Strategic Communications Branch. Ministers could be supported in their work by special advisers. In practice, however, these were appointed to a centralised Policy Unit by the First Minister in an attempt to overcome the type of inter-departmental rivalries - fuelled by 'spin doctors' and 'policy wonks' - which had dogged the Blair government. The advisers would be eligible to participate alongside civil servants and representatives of external organisations in the work of ministerial committees and working groups, established to deal with issues spanning portfolios or requiring collective consideration. In the event, eight of these bodies were set up, including ministerial working groups on Section 28 and student finance, ministerial committees on digital Scotland, drug misuse and rural development, and a poverty and inclusion task force.

The machinery of government functioned fairly smoothly during the first year. Despite some potentially divisive issues, the working relationship between Dewar and Wallace was sound (surviving its most serious test over the issue of student fees) while the Cabinet and the other ministerial bodies operated effectively on the basis of genuine collective decision-making. Ironically, as noted below, trouble arose from one part of the system which had been specifically designed to prevent political embarrassments: the Policy Unit containing special advisers and led initially by John Rafferty as chief-of-staff.

# THE EXECUTIVE AND THE PARLIAMENT

The Executive quickly settled into a formal routine of reporting its activities to the Parliament through the medium of a weekly Question Time. From January 2000 this session was focussed specifically on the person of Donald Dewar, in the First Minister's Question Time. Additionally, Ministers were regularly asked to appear before the sixteen parliamentary committees set up to scrutinise the policy, legislation, finance and administration of the Scottish Executive. Some tensions developed in the relationship between the Executive and these committees. When Susan Deacon, the Minister for Health and Community Care, and Rhona Brankin, the Deputy Minister for Culture and Sport, were criticised following their appearances before parliamentary committees in November 1999, the First Minister stepped into the fray (Hardie, 1999; Scott, 1999). Delivering the annual John P. Macintosh lecture, Dewar criticised the committees developing practice of routinely calling Ministers before them: 'It must not become the norm. Committee agendas should not be dominated by the morning's headlines and their potential for spawning press releases' (Hardie, 1999).

Some opposition MSPs, including Mike Russell, the SNP business manager and a member of the Education, Culture and Sport Committee, claimed this was Executive interference in the legitimate role of the Parliament (Hardie, 1999). Impartial observers probably drew the conclusion that a Parliament worthy of the name will seek to keep ministers under close scrutiny.

## IMPACT AND IMAGE: SOME TRENDS

It was perhaps inevitable that the teething problems of devolution would create an element of strain in the relationship between the First Minister and the Scottish Executive on the one hand, and Westminster and Whitehall on the other. Those who had predicted trouble between Edinburgh and London were given some opportunities to claim vindication during the first year. However, it might be argued that tension between the centre and devolved institutions is a natural, inherent element of any devolution settlement, and management of this tension was always going to be a key challenge for the First Minister and the Executive. Of greater concern was the fact that some of the tensions between Edinburgh and London, and indeed between the Executive and the Parliament, had less to do with policy as such, than with the handling of a series of crises which dogged the First Minister and the Executive for part of the year.

As the Scottish Executive and the Scotland Office settled into new working arrangements, a highly publicised 'turf war' appeared to break out between the First Minister and the Secretary of State for Scotland (see, for example, Dinwoodie, 1999), although much of this was symbolic in nature (based on arguments about the residual scale and importance of the Secretary of State's 'empire'). This matter was settled fairly quickly, partly due to the prevailing good sense of Donald Dewar and John Reid, and in retrospect it came to be seen as something of a storm in a teacup.

The real implications of devolution started to be brought home to Prime Minister Blair as examples grew of policy divergence between Edinburgh and London on such issues as aid to farmers, ending the ban on 'beef on the bone', replacing student fees, and marginally more adventurous freedom of information legislation. While he professed to be relaxed about such matters, Blair's capacity to tolerate less than complete control over an element of the system of government was undoubtedly tested.

As the months passed, mechanisms were introduced (and new ones proposed) with the aim of bringing about the maximum degree of policy convergence consistent with genuine devolution. The ground rules for co-operation and communication, and the broad working relations between Whitehall departments and the Scottish administration were set out in concordats which were finally published in October 1999. As part of this framework, a Joint Ministerial Committee (JMC) was set up, to meet normally once a year in order to consider issues affecting different parts of the UK and attempt to resolve any disputes. The JMC would be chaired by the Prime Minister (or his representative) and consist of the Deputy Prime Minister, the Scottish First Minister and one of his ministerial colleagues, the Welsh First Secretary, the Northern Ireland First Minister and his Deputy, and the Secretaries of State for Scotland, Wales and Northern Ireland. The relatively loose, non-statutory framework of the concordats and the JMC would have been tightened under a proposal mooted by Gordon Brown at the end of November 1999. The Chancellor of the Exchequer argued for the establishment of formal joint sub-committees of the UK Cabinet which would involve Ministers from the Scottish Executive and Whitehall working together on key policy issues (Nicolson, 1999). The opposition parties reacted negatively to what appeared to be a 'kite-flying' exercise which nonetheless raised the serious question of where the line should be drawn between legitimate spheres of responsibility under the devolution settlement.

The palpable successes of the First Secretary and the Executive during their first year have to be set against the way they struggled to cope with the bad publicity which accompanied a series of crises. These included:

- the Ruddle scandal, which resulted in the release of a psychopathic killer on a legal technicality.
- the 'Lobbygate' affair, which involved allegations that key special advisers were negotiating privileged access for certain PR firms and lobbyists.
- a failure to anticipate some of the complexities arising from implementation

of the European Convention on Human Rights - hence the debacle surrounding suspension of the temporary Sheriffs.

- a miscalculation of the reaction in some quarters to repeal of Section 28. This miscalculation forced the Executive into crisis management in the face of an unexpectedly strong campaign against the proposed repeal and created some friction within the Executive. It is worth noting that policy management lessons were drawn from this affair. A new ministerial working group was created to develop a response strategy not only to the campaign against abolition but also to the attack on 'other social reforms' favoured by the Executive.
- the enforced resignation of the First Minister's chief-of-staff John Rafferty in the wake of accusations that he had misled the media.
- the departure of the senior adviser in charge of the Strategic Communications branch, Philip Chalmers, following drink-related motoring convictions.
- the sudden departure of Lord Hardie, the Lord Advocate, in February 2000 just before the trial of the Lockerbie suspects was about to start in the Netherlands.

The poor performance of both coalition partners in the first by-election of the Scottish Parliament, at Ayr in March 2000, was indicative of the public's general disenchantment with the Executive's handling of these matters. The First Minister was undoubtedly unfortunate to face a sequence of sudden crises which sorely tested his responsiveness. It might be argued that greater foresight and some improved luck, coupled with more assured reactions when crises do occur, would ensure there was no repetition of these PR disasters.

## CONCLUSION

Observers can only speculate in broad terms about the likely or desirable developments in this sphere between the end of the first year of operation of the First Minister and the Scottish Executive and the end of the first Parliament in 2003. However, it seems probable that some clarification will emerge in a number of key areas.

For example, we might hope to see the Executive embrace the consequences of the implementation of a new culture of openness and accessibility, coupled with an enhanced Executive accountability which should accompany the advent of a new audit regime based on the creation of Audit Scotland and the post of Auditor General and the growing maturity and experience of the parliamentary committees.

Evidence of a greater degree of strategic thought in relation to some policy developments, and a surer touch when handling the inevitable crises of government life, would be welcome, not least within the ranks of the Executive itself. One suggested approach is the appointment of a designated political (as opposed to government) deputy to the First Minister, to take some of the strain off Dewar (Brown, 2000). This issue was brought into clear focus in May 2000 when the First Minister underwent heart surgery and it was announced that he would be spending up to 12 weeks away from his post recuperating.

The working relations between Edinburgh and London will, and should, become clearer as the concordats take real effect, the JMC becomes fully operational and the long-term future of the Scotland Office and the post of Secretary of State is settled (perhaps through the creation of a new 'Constitutional Affairs' department which would help to rationalise roles and relationships in Scottish governance but at the loss of a dedicated Scottish seat in the UK Cabinet).

The character of the Executive might alter as a consequence of the ministerial reshuffles which are bound to take place over the next three years. Less desirable will be the destabilising effect of any manoeuvring for position to succeed Donald Dewar as the next Scottish parliamentary election approaches. As news of the First Minister's health problems emerged on the eve of the Parliament's first anniversary, politicians and pundits started to speculate abut his eventual successor.

# my visit to the scottish parliament

## laura brown

I found our visit to the Scottish Parliament very interesting. On the Thursday when we got there we had our lunch, the food was great - a real buffet! Then we split into our workshops and did some role play, a lady professor gave us a fright by telling us about a meteorite that was heading our way in three weeks time. Our job was to try and figure out what we could do to save the earth! What a responsibility!

After some fun we went to the Scottish Parliament to test our mikes and our voting system. During the night we could not sleep as we were too excited about Friday. When Friday came we ate all our breakfast and went to our seats in the Scottish Parliament (with David Steel and other nice MSPs). We voted a lot but it was fun. The best day of all was all done.

The next day was Saturday. A huge big trip to Dynamic Earth. The ground shaked and moved, the iceberg was cold! We went to the shop and bought lots of treats like chocolate bars and big bags of sweets.

My trip to Edinburgh was so good. No it was not just good, it was fantastic!

# CHAPTER 10: the civil service and the scottish executive's structure and style

**richard parry**

At the root of the civil service's behaviour during the first year of devolution is their understanding that the widely-shared perception amongst civil servants as now 'working for the Scottish Parliament' was not correct. The Executive's officials knew that their constitutional status had not changed. They remained part of the Home Civil Service and so tied in to Whitehall management and personnel systems, especially for the grades in the Senior Civil Service; and the relation between legislature and executive in Scotland was the same as at Westminster. With the backing of the First Minister, they pursued a path of continuity from the Scottish Office, especially in organisational structure. During the year they were buffeted by a vast increase in workload as they serviced three times as many Ministers and twice as many parliamentarians without much of a summer break in 1999. They also had to suffer leaked criticism that Ministers were expecting more of them and did not appreciate the old style of service they were receiving. By the end of the year Ministers and officials were adjusting to each other and taking forward a lively style of 'joined-up' policy making on the issues, but it had been a rougher ride than most of them had expected.

The devolution transition was used as a time of maintenance rather than a time of opportunity by the civil service because of an imbalance between the parliamentary and the official preparation. The Consultative Steering Group (CSG) on the Scottish Parliament had an extended time-scale, incorporation of outside expertise, building up the recommendations from first principles, and a desire to set a presumed open, accessible and inclusive world against the presumed closed world of Westminster (Consultative Steering Group, 1999). Where the CSG set down detail, it has tended to be followed. A good example of this adherence is the influence of the Financial Issues Advisory Group, which recommended a three-stage process of parliamentary approval of spending plans that has taken the devolved administration some way ahead of Treasury traditions of Budget secrecy. Here we had an example of Scotland as a pace-setter in administrative reform (one embraced by the retired Treasury official who sat on the group); in many other aspects of the reform of the executive branch there was no external frame of reference, no road map to follow. Where the CSG was silent, a default position of replication of the Scottish Office and of Westminster/Whitehall was the result.

## PROCESSES AND PERSONALITIES

An obvious question to arise therefore was why there was no 'CSG Mark II' covering the decision-making processes of the Executive and the relations of the civil service to ministers and MSPs. Part of the answer which should be emphasised was the lack of time in the exercise. The Scottish Administration Steering Group (the planning mechanism in the Scottish Office) started work only in December 1998, by which time it had to concentrate on an action plan - Preparing to be the Scottish Executive - that was an inventory of the issues needing to be addressed to keep the show on the road. Senior officials looked at alternative organisational models in autumn 1998, with the temporary help of Terry Kirchin, a seconded senior BP manager, but quickly concluded that the shape of the Scottish Office should be preserved as much as possible. In this decision they were influenced by the volume of routine business for which continuity had to be maintained across the devolution transition.

It would never have been easy to move towards civil service reform in parallel with everything else that was happening in 1998 (including the pre-emption of much time and energy by the Parliament building project). There was little advance knowledge of whom the new Ministers would be and how they would wish to do their jobs. Other parties laid out a suggested structure of ministries, but Labour's manifesto was silent and their pre-election intelligence sketchy and in the event not very accurate. The politicians did not want a 'CSG Mark II' and were happy to reproduce a conventional government versus opposition arrangement. Officials naturally concurred with this approach and took the opportunity to carry forward the Scottish Office in a technically proficient but politically unimaginative way.

Another line of understanding is to look at the interaction of the two dominant personalities in the exercise: the First Minister Donald Dewar and the Permanent Secretary Muir Russell. Donald Dewar has never been preoccupied with structural variables inside government; he is notoriously unconcerned with image; and his style is attractively unsystematic. Therefore much fell to the

Permanent Secretary, a likeable star long tipped for the highest office but for whom the post came a little too late (May 1998) to let him stamp fully his own imprint on devolution planning. He did some important things, especially to establish under the guise of the Management Group Support Staff an embryonic policy unit of civil servants that was able to dovetail with the Executive's special advisers in a Policy Unit headed by an adviser (Brian Fitzpatrick). Russell also took a high profile with staff, giving speeches at roadshows, putting out upbeat messages and sponsoring a 'DevCom' communications exercise. He set the membership of the Scottish Administration Steering Group to include some younger officials and exclude all but one of the heads of department. But generally he did not seek to impose on the heads of department his apparent interest in business-derived methods and in thinking emerging from Whitehall.

What Russell also did - with Dewar's blessing - was to set in place a 'dual centre' for the office. One part is an Executive Secretariat under Robert Gordon (the leading devolution planner, promoted to head of department rank in December 1998) and including functions such as legal services and information that go wider than a Cabinet Secretariat. The other is the collection of finance, personnel and corporate services functions remaining under their own heads and reporting directly to the Permanent Secretary. Both Gordon and Russell attend the Cabinet. Russell also made the surprisingly bold decision to split the Education and Industry Department in advance of the election rather than do the expected thing of leaving the matter to the incoming administration (which in the event split it in a different way). The motive here seemed to be the need to set in train the recruitment of an extra departmental head.

Post-devolution, Donald Dewar endorsed the Scottish Office practice of taking the structure of departments as fixed rather than defining ministerial responsibilities and designing departments around them. Sarah Boyack was not given a Transport and Environment Department of her own; Jack McConnell's important responsibilities at the centre, including finance and personnel, were not brought together in one organisation; and the Development Department was left working with three Cabinet Ministers. Two departments changed in name only: Agriculture, Fisheries and Environment became Rural Affairs, and Home became Justice (without absorbing the Crown Office and Lord Advocate's Department). Next Steps agencies were maintained. Even the letterheads and building signs showed minimal change.

# THE TRANSITION

For the civil service, a transition process is bound to be a mixture of correct and incorrect calls. The most useful correct calls were that the Scottish Executive could be used as the brand name of the new administration and that Ministers would be happy for it to retain (for reasons of economy) the design image of the Scottish Office; that the 'tight ship' style of new Labour would be in accord with civil service wishes not to break up central services functions and create ministries; and that officials should be on hand to assist the partnership negotiations between Labour and Liberal Democrats. The incorrect ones were on the number of Ministers (meaning that accommodation and staffing were not ready for all 22 appointees), on the split between education and industry, and on the prominence of the office of the Secretary of State for Scotland.

These three incorrect calls made the transition period between May 17th (when the Executive was formed) and July 1st 1999 (when it assumed its functions) a difficult one. Officials had not fully grasped that during the period their strict line of authority was to John Reid, rather than Donald Dewar and the new Ministers. Reid understandably wanted more than the minimal number of support staff he had been allocated under the plans and also offices in Edinburgh and Glasgow to put them in. The fact that higher education as well as industry would move to a Glasgow-based department (Enterprise and Lifelong Learning) was a serious obstacle to personnel and accommodation management, especially after John Reid gained a foothold in Meridian Court, the Executive's Glasgow building.

Avoidance of 'departmentalitis' through the retention of Executive-wide finance, personnel and information groups was a major achievement. At a time when Whitehall has been struggling to break up the 'baronies' and 'silos' that grind against each other in the Cabinet system, St Andrew's House resisted much slippage, the exception being the carving-up of the Social Work Service group among education, health and justice. During the autumn 1999 expenditure round, finance officials continued to serve both Jack McConnell and the Minister in their spending area, and the office continued to be a unified personnel system. This extends to the coalition aspects; the civil service has guided a way of incorporating Ministers of a minority party into British conventions of collective responsibility and decision-making

Many officials have not been quite up to speed or in tune with what modern Ministers, rightly or wrongly, are expecting of them. Officials have drawn upon their Scottish Office role model of Ministers and have often not been comfortable with the intense, media-driven, output-orientated style of some of the younger Ministers, Wendy Alexander being most often cited in this regard. Ministers have not been easy to house-train in matters such as fixing of diaries, stability of physical location, accepting drafts for signature and the conventions about direct dealing with more junior officials. The predominance of fiftysomething males in the senior civil service ranks must also have an effect.

But we have seen a tentative movement towards a pattern of civil service behaviour more consistent with the spirit of CSG than with traditional Whitehall norms. The initial instinct was to codify relationships with the Parliament, in matters such as the provision of information to MSPs, the handling of requests from the Scottish Parliament Information Centre, the arrangements of briefings for MSPs, the appearance of civil servants before parliamentary committees, and the duties and accountabilities of officials. The problem is that written statements in these areas will tend to be cautious and Westminster-like. They have not accorded with the reality of Holyrood life, with its greater informality, lesser anonymity and easier contact between civil servants and parliamentary staff (with many of the latter moving from the Scottish Office and on close terms with their former colleagues). The parliamentary committees and the civil service are slowly learning a more collaborative style for the exchange of information.

## FUTURE ISSUES

For the future, two issues stand out: the suggestion of a policy-making deficit in the civil service, and the indispensability or otherwise of continued membership of the Home Civil Service. The first was raised in a cogent way by John Rafferty in a speech to Executive Secretariat officials a few days before his departure as Donald Dewar's chief of staff - the essence of which was reported later in The *Herald* (Brogan, 1999). A problem here is that the media have consistently been seeking confirmation of the civil service as a group of unreconstructed Sir Humphreys and missed the apparently more balanced tone of what Rafferty said to the staff. The media have also sought to portray, against the evidence, Rafferty's dismissal as the product of a civil service plot. But Rafferty's line still has a logic: the officials give their Ministers servility, but not an imaginative consideration of what Ministers are trying to do. Officials are the masters of the technicalities of the game, but do not get to grips with the way that policy outputs are to be achieved and real differences made.

The second issue is the future of the Whitehall base of the Scottish Civil Service. Continued membership of the Home Civil Service is written into the Scotland Act and is claimed, explicitly, to facilitate movement within British central government and access to expertise, and, implicitly, to be the guarantor of the impartiality and integrity of officials. In practice, this has kept the most senior officials in the Whitehall web of committees and working parties, especially under the rubric of *Modernising Government*, the policies which since a White Paper of March 1999 have sought to make the civil service more open, accessible and skilled at policy implementation. For modernisers - probably including Muir Russell - this has proved a useful vehicle for introducing new ideas and in some respects fills the gap caused by the lack of a 'CSG Mark II'. The Scottish Executive's 'joined-up' policy-making featured prominently in the Cabinet Office's document of January 2000, *Wiring It Up* (Performance and Innovation Unit of the Cabinet Office, 2000). The constitutional issue remains of whether these initiatives could ever impose policy constraints on the Executive.

The second aspect of the Home Civil Service is the psychological one of being 'at home' and 'in the club'. A long-standing theme of devolution is that it should not be like local government writ large, a line of thought sliding into 'the more like UK central government the better'. Fear of provincialism, like fear of nationalism, can run very deep. Senior Executive officials seem to be going to Whitehall more, not less, often in order to assert their place at the top table. Staff transfers into the Executive have imported more, not less, blood from Whitehall (though it should be noted that the import of senior staff from non-civil service backgrounds is on the agenda, and a competition for that purpose took place in early 2000).

During the transition, staff were protected from the full impact of the constitutional journey that they were embarking upon by reassurances about the continuity of practices and values from the old to the new. These practices have been based upon some deeply embedded understandings about the proper ways for civil servants to behave to Ministers, parliamentarians, the rest of the public sector, the media and the public at large. But these understandings extend to the proper behaviour of those on the other side of the exchange as well, and some officials have felt disappointed.

The Scottish system may be edging towards the Welsh situation in which the 'team' incorporates executive and legislature, and serving Ministers is not construed as declining to serve everyone else. This is going to require changes of mentality by civil servants. They might have saved themselves a lot of trouble by taking the spirit of CSG on board during 1999 and not holding so jealously on to the reproduction of their previous values and structures. The cautious strategy they chose makes some sense. There was no time to think everything through, and not enough interest from Ministers in administrative change. The show stayed on the road in the short term; in the longer-term, new concepts based on post-devolution circumstances will be demanded of the civil service and Ministers.

# END NOTE

The research reported here was conducted with the assistance of Amy Jones and funded by the Economic and Social Research Council as part of its Devolution and Institutional Change Initiative, ref L327253015. We are most grateful to senior civil servants of the Executive for agreeing to be interviewed during the project.

# the implications of cubie

## lindsay paterson

The controversy over student finance arose in 1997, when the Westminster Education Secretary, David Blunkett, introduced student fees in higher education, and replaced the remaining student grants with loans. This was criticised throughout the UK, most vocally for the breach of what was claimed to be a 'principle of free education', even though the biggest impact on students came from the ending of grants. In Scotland, the May 1999 elections produced a parliamentary majority opposed to fees, because only Labour supported the new arrangement in full. Rather than face an immediate vote for abolition, Labour conceded a committee of inquiry during the coalition negotiations, to be chaired by Andrew Cubie, a lawyer and former chair of CBI Scotland who had won widespread admiration for his work in the Consultative Steering Group on the Parliament's working practices.

The committee's report in December 1999 recommended the ending of fees, and a requirement that well-paid graduates would pay into an endowment fund that would be used to re-introduce grants for poor students. The government accepted most of the principles, though in an attenuated form: both the threshold for graduates' payment, and the level of the grants, were set at a lower level than Cubie wanted. But up-front fees were abolished, and about half of graduates would be exempt from payment altogether - those who, when they were students, were on diploma courses, were aged over 21, were lone parents, or were disabled. Controversially, these new arrangements would apply only to Scottish and non-UK EU students attending institutions in Scotland: excluded would be Scottish students at other UK institutions and non-Scottish UK students at Scottish institutions.

This episode is of wider significance for four reasons. It showed the effect of proportional elections: Labour could not get its own way. It inaugurated a consultative style of policy-making: Cubie and his committee broke new ground in the thoroughness with which they sought evidence. It invented a new source of revenue for the Parliament: the graduate endowment payment is not a tax, and yet provides income from mostly well-off people that the government proposes to redistribute to the poor. Above all, the report enunciated a philosophy of social democratic redistribution that was accepted in principle by almost every segment of Scottish opinion, and marks a sharp break from the dominant fiscal conservatism of policy in England.

# CHAPTER 11: the financial powers of the scottish parliament

## sheila dow and
## david bell

Finance is key to the operation of the Scottish Parliament. All of the spending departments - Enterprise and Lifelong Learning, Health, Justice, Rural Affairs, Development and Education - require finance to carry out their programmes. The greater the funding that is available, the more readily objectives can be met. But the funds that the Scottish Parliament receives are limited by the size of the grant that it receives from Westminster, determined by the Barnett Formula. This is the same mechanism that has existed since the late 1970s, when it was named after the then First Secretary to the Treasury - Joel Barnett. The formula determines the change in block grant from the previous year, based on a fixed proportion of the change in spending in England on those functions devolved to Scotland. The proportion is based on population shares, last revised in 1992.

There is one other potential source of revenue - the tax varying power that has been granted to the Parliament. This would allow the Scottish Parliament to vary the basic rate of income tax by up to three pence in the pound. However, the ruling Labour-Lib Dem coalition closed this option off during the first Parliament. Even if it were introduced, the revenue that it would raise would only be a small fraction of the Westminster block grant to Scotland.

Thus the new Scottish Parliament receives broadly the same amount of resources from Westminster as did the Scottish Office in pre-devolution times. It is generally accepted that this settlement has been generous to Scotland in financial terms. In particular, it has enabled successive Scottish administrations to spend more per head on certain key services, such as health and education, than has been possible in England and Wales. How generous the settlement has been in terms of relative needs is less clear; if needs per head are higher in Scotland than in England, then a higher allocation per head could be justified (McCrone, 1999). But this question cannot be answered without a proper exercise in assessing relative needs throughout the UK. However, regardless of relative needs, the implications of the mathematics underlying the Barnett Formula is that eventually public spending per head will be equalised over all parts of the UK. While this will not happen in the foreseeable future, it does seem likely that the block grant from Westminster will gradually appear to be less generous than is currently the case. This is the phenomenon known as the 'Barnett squeeze' (see Midwinter, 1999 for an alternative perspective).

## BARNETT AND PROBLEMS FOR THE PARLIAMENT

Though the Barnett Formula is often viewed as somewhat arcane, it has the power to cause very real problems for the devolved Parliament. The difficulty is that the credibility of the Parliament with the electorate relies on its ability to deliver effective public services. But the Barnett squeeze implies that even if these services are growing in real terms, they will not be growing as rapidly in Scotland as they will in England and Wales.

In the last budget, the UK government promised substantially more resources for education and particularly for health. Scotland will receive its share of these increases and consequently the Parliament will be able to increase spending on health and education, should it wish. Two difficulties immediately arise.

First, Westminster Budget announcements will create expectations among the Scottish electorate that similar improvements will be delivered in Scotland as are being promised to England and Wales. Acceding to these wishes creates the impression that the Parliament is merely a transmission mechanism for Westminster policy. Adopting a different approach to allocating resources may alienate the electorate if the Westminster spending plans have widespread popular support in Scotland, as is probably true with the increased spending on health and education. (In the longer term, the climate at Westminster could change such that spending in devolved areas could be reduced, creating different problems for Scotland.)

Second, even if there are absolute improvements in provision in Scotland, the Barnett squeeze will ensure that increases in Scotland are relatively smaller than those in England and Wales. In essence this means that the opposition parties in the Scottish Parliament will be able to complain that though health and education spending in Scotland has increased, increases in England and Wales have been more rapid.

# SPENDING AND PROVISION: AN IMPORTANT DISTINCTION IN PUBLIC SERVICES

However, one must be careful to distinguish between spending on public services and their provision. The former is an input in the production of public services, while the latter is the output of this process. The arguments in favour of the establishment of the Scottish Parliament have to do with provision of public services, not with public spending. In particular, prior to devolution, expectations were raised that a Scottish Parliament would:

- provide a range of public services to more accurately reflect the wishes of the Scottish people;
- enable public services in Scotland to be produced more efficiently and thus release resources to other civic priorities.

So far, the Executive has concentrated on the first of these tasks. It has embarked on a consultation process over spending priorities with some enthusiasm. In April 2000, Jack McConnell, as Finance Minister announced that he wished to engage in a comprehensive consultation process across the nation the like of which had never been seen before, on the priorities for spending within the £17.7bn budget.

The idea that there would be much greater consultation over spending priorities in a devolved Scotland was anticipated in the FIAG (Financial Issues Advisory Group) report. The Secretary of State for Scotland set up FIAG in February 1998 with the task of proposing rules, procedures, standing orders and legislation for the handling of financial issues by the Scottish Parliament. This report heavily influenced the subsequent consultation paper on the financial framework for the Scottish Parliament. Subsequently the Public Finance and Accountability (Scotland) Act 2000 was passed which lays out procedures for audit and accountability. The intention of this framework was to:

- give the people of Scotland a say in how their money is spent;
- provide the financial information needed for effective decision making;
- ensure that the Scottish Executive is accountable to the Parliament and to the people of Scotland;
- provide an independent and vigorous audit system and value for money regime.

The first of these aims has been incorporated into the annual budget process. This begins with the publication each spring of a report on how the Scottish Executive has spent its money in past years and how it intends to spend it in the future. The second stage of the budget process is to prepare a draft budget for 2001-02 which will be presented to Parliament in the autumn for further consultation. The final stage of the process is the preparation, consideration and enactment of a Budget Bill around January or February of the following year.

This is a clearly open process - especially given Jack McConnell's initiative. However, there is some scepticism as to how far it will result in deviations from the Executive's published spending plans. The block grant from Westminster to the Executive is fixed and there is very limited scope for borrowing. Inevitably most submissions will be suggestions for increased spending. With a fixed spending limit, increases cannot be made under one heading unless there is a corresponding reduction elsewhere. These will be particularly difficult if they involve re-allocations between departments, and Ministers are intent on protecting their original allocations.

One example of this problem is the way in which the Executive dealt with the report of the Cubie Committee (Independent Committee of Inquiry into Student Funding, 1999). The change to the student finance system recommended by the Executive implied additional costs of £33m. This money has been found from within the budget of the Department of Enterprise and Lifelong Learning, thus ensuring that no other Departments were disadvantaged by the outcome. If a carefully considered and costed report with substantial popular support, such as that produced by the Cubie Committee did not result in re-allocation between Department heads, it is difficult to imagine that less thoroughly researched proposals from the public and special interest groups could have a more substantial effect.

Thus, the Executive has begun with very modest changes to the ways that it allocates resources within Scotland. More radical change may come as the Parliament grows in confidence, but the forces likely to resist change should not be under-estimated. First there is the argument, particularly strong if the Westminster government is popular, that Scottish spending priorities should not substantially deviate from those in the rest of the UK. Second, there will be understandable resistance from those that are adversely affected by change.

# THE FUTURE OF PUBLIC SERVICE FINANCING?

Nevertheless, there are a range of policy areas in which the Parliament might wish to consider the distribution of finance to produce more effective and equitable public services. One area where major change was being considered before the establishment of the Parliament was health. The Arbuthnott Committee report *Fair Shares for All* (Scottish Executive, 1999a) suggested that equality of access to healthcare would be promoted by changes that would effectively re-allocate funding towards the West of Scotland, which has an appallingly poor health record. In fact, the Health Committee of the Parliament responded negatively to the report and the future of this initiative is at present uncertain.

There are many other areas that the Parliament might wish to examine the way in which it distributes finance. For example, the Parliament might want to consider whether or not the current structure of local enterprise companies is effective and efficient. It might assess whether or not the university structure could be changed to make it more relevant to Scotland's needs. It might deliberate the balance between the resources allocated to secondary and primary education. It could also examine the success of the present local authority structure in delivering the services that local people need at a reasonable cost. In short, it is important that the Parliament understands the concept of 'opportunity cost', so beloved of economists. If the financial resources over which the Parliament has control are not being put to their most effective use, then an opportunity is being lost to improve the circumstances of some individual or group of people in Scotland.

# glasgow: time for change

## douglas robertson

Since the war, numerous plans and schemes have been drawn up for Glasgow's renewal and have been implemented. To eradicate unacceptable levels of poverty and poor housing, Glasgow needed to undergo some radical surgery. Heavy industry, long in decline, was to be replaced by consumer focused manufacturing, located in the emerging New Towns and specified development areas. Vast rehousing programmes were also required to eradicate the tenement slums and support skilled labour migration to the New Towns. So while the Clyde Valley Plan of 1949 outlined the vision, it was the Scottish Council's Toothill Report of 1961 which provided the strategy. But has the radical surgery improved the patient's chances?

Glasgow's population has fallen from 1.05 million to just 611,000 since 1951; the real level of unemployment stood at 30.4 per cent in 1997, as opposed to the 'official' rate of 13.8 per cent; between 1971 and 1996 employment in Glasgow fell by 25 per cent and in manufacturing by 74 per cent. Out of the UK's 17 largest cities, Glasgow has the lowest rate of working age employment at 56 per cent. And things are not getting any better - economic activity fell by 5 per cent between 1993-9. But does not old Glasgow look well with all the new shops, hotels and call centre jobs. Do not talk the patient down, because if this remedy is failing there will not be anything else. Best stick with the panoply of palliative remedies, now neatly repacked by the Glasgow Alliance, Donald Dewar's only concession to his native city's chronic and deteriorating condition. Improving council houses via private funding solutions may ameliorate certain symptoms, but in the long term it could result in a continuation of a rent regime that demands welfare dependence.

Why is it no one in the Executive sees fit to address the city's chronic unemployment and abject poverty? With over half of Scotland's working age benefits claimants resident in the city, prioritising employment creation within Glasgow could radically reduce Scotland's poverty level. Why is no one in the Parliament asking searching questions about Glasgow's prognosis and treatment? It will not be easy to get the Executive to admit that the government's long-standing policy towards Glasgow is now the cause of so many of the city's problems. It will be even harder to challenge the long established power systems, and associated elites, who continue to manage Scotland despite the advent of the Parliament.

# CHAPTER 12: the modernisation of the scottish legal system: a work in progress

## lynne macmillan

The Scottish Parliament assumed its powers on July 1st 1999, a day marked by a considerable amount of optimism and celebration in Edinburgh and throughout Scotland. One of the expectations for the Parliament, expressed by many but probably most typically by the Scottish Constitutional Convention was as follows:

> *One of the greatest anomalies which the creation of a Scottish Parliament will put to rights concerns Scots law. Scotland is the only democratic country in the world with its own system of law but no legislature of its own to determine that law. Scotland has a legal system which is quite different from that of the rest of the UK, yet under the Westminster system it is legislated for by a Parliament outwith Scotland and one in which only a small minority represent Scottish constituencies.*
>
> **(Scottish Constitutional Convention, 1995: 15)**

The correction of this anomaly was a significant reason why many concerned about the state of our legal system looked forward to the establishment of the Scottish Parliament. Along with the Scottish Constitutional Convention, the Law Society of Scotland, civic organisations, charities, public bodies and professional associations in Scotland had looked on while changes were made to the English legal system which helped to improve the capability of the law to regulate people's affairs. While not all changes would have been welcomed in Scotland, there was certainly a broad perception that certain aspects of the Scottish legal system had a neglected air about them. In particular, some of the areas of law which had received thorough and detailed attention by the Scottish Law Commission, but the areas concerned were not of enough political significance to be given parliamentary time at Westminster. A Scottish Parliament would allow proper attention to be paid to the modernisation of Scotland's law and legal system.

This chapter will consider some of the more significant developments in the Scottish legal system since the establishment of the Scottish Parliament in May 1999. It is not possible to provide a comprehensive summary, but nevertheless it is hoped that an impression will be gained that a considerable step forward has been made in the task of ensuring that the Scottish legal system is fit for the twenty-first century.

When we talk about the Scottish legal system, we encompass common law of Scotland (which includes the decisions of judges in court cases, and the certain legal writings which are regarded as authoritative) and most importantly, legislation. Legislation includes statutes passed by the Westminster Parliament, also now the Scottish Parliament, and European Union legislation, which is usually incorporated into our system by a Westminster or Scottish Parliament statute. Also included is subordinate legislation, which are regulations and other rules which are authorised by the UK or Scottish Parliament. This chapter will concentrate on significant court decisions as well as legislative change.

The reorganisation of ministerial responsibilities in the Scottish Executive created a Minister for Justice, who at present is Jim Wallace, leader of the Scottish Liberal Democrats, and Deputy First Minister for Scotland. He is supported by a Deputy Minister for Justice, the Labour MSP for Edinburgh South. The Home Department in the old Scottish Office became the Justice Department in the Scottish Executive. The change also brought the Scottish Courts Administration formally within the Department. The Justice Department is also the department to which the Prison Service and the Scottish Court Service are accountable. The Minister for Justice shares some responsibilities with the Lord Advocate, who is responsible for prosecuting crime generally, through the Crown Office and the Crown Agent.

## THE NATURE OF CHANGE IN THE FIRST YEAR

The changes to the legal system which took place in the Scottish Parliament's first year were significant, especially if one considers the relative pace of change in Scotland before the establishment of the Parliament. The impact of those statutory changes will be progressively appreciated as the legislation passed in the first and subsequent years of the Scottish Parliament are brought into force. The impact of court decisions, for example, in relation to temporary sheriffs, made an immediate impact.

# LEGISLATION

Fundamentally, a Parliament exists to pass laws, so the best place to start describing the changes that have occurred in the legal system is to consider which new laws have been passed which relate to the legal system.

The Scottish Parliament's first legislative programme was announced on June 16th 1999. A list of eight separate pieces of legislation were unveiled by First Minister Donald Dewar, and the details of the complete programme are covered separately in this book by Peter Jones (see Chapter Seven). The most significant pieces of legislation in relation to the legal system which have now been passed by the Scottish Parliament, are the Abolition of Feudal Tenure etc. (Scotland) Bill and the Adults with Incapacity (Scotland) Bill, and further discussion of them will be included here.

There have been other significant legislative changes in the last year in the Scottish Parliament which were not included in the Scottish Executive's legislative programme, which will also be discussed briefly, and these include the initiatives by backbench MSPs of the Scottish Parliament, through private members' legislation.

## THE ABOLITION OF FEUDAL TENURE ETC. (SCOTLAND) BILL

Scotland's ancient feudal land tenure system had been earmarked for complete abolition rather than reform, since at least the 1970s. Feudal tenure is a system of landownership which has existed in Scotland for many hundreds of years, and is generally regarded as outmoded, archaic and unfair. While legislation was introduced in the 1970s to remove some of its worst effects, the feudal system itself has remained. The Scottish Law Commission published a discussion paper in 1991 inviting comments on its proposals for abolition (Scottish Law Commission, 1991), followed by a Report in February 1999, which attached a draft bill (Scottish Law Commission, 1999). It is a classic case of a Scots law reform measure which had never made it to the top of the list of priorities for parliamentary time at Westminster.

The legislation to abolish the feudal system was finally approved by the Scottish Parliament on May 3rd 2000. On a date still to be determined (but it is likely to be approximately two years after the legislation receives Royal Assent), the feudal system will be abolished, and replaced by a system of outright landownership with suitable protections to ensure that it will continue to be possible to maintain common facilities, such as shared gardens, and to protect the amenity of property. A system of compensation is provided for the owners of superiority rights to obtain compensation for the loss of such rights.

This piece of legislation is highly technical and is more likely, in its detailed aspects, to be of interest to conveyancing solicitors than to members of the general public. However, it did become a focus for a considerable amount of attention because of the activities of those interested in the wider implications of land reform in Scotland.

The Scottish Land Reform Convention, and others, have for many years been raising awareness of the importance of ownership of land from the point of view of ecological stewardship. At issue was whether or not the Crown, as 'guardian of the public interest', should be allowed to retain paramount superiority in order to act on behalf of the people of Scotland to ensure that private landowners acted responsibly in their ownership. This issue has, indeed, dominated much of the debate in committee and in the chamber debates of the new Parliament. These arguments were resisted, ultimately successfully, by the Scottish Executive, who considered the legislation to be simply a technical measure to tidy up Scottish conveyancing law.

## THE ADULTS WITH INCAPACITY (SCOTLAND) BILL

Another piece of legislation long anticipated by those involved in the particular field was the Adults with Incapacity (Scotland) Bill. The new law will reform the law regulating how the financial and other affairs of people suffering from mental incapacity are dealt with. It had been recognised by the Scottish Law Commission in their 1995 Report and draft Bill on Incapable Adults that the present law was failing to meet the welfare and financial needs of adults with incapacity.

It is estimated that around 100,000 Scots lack capacity for whatever reason in some or all areas of their lives. Adults with incapacity can be people with a mental incapacity, including those suffering from dementia or a severe learning disability, or they may have had a stroke or head injury, and cannot make or communicate their own decisions.

The measures being introduced by the legislation include:

- The appointment of attorneys and guardians to look after financial and welfare matters.
- Legally authorising banks, building societies and others to release funds from the account of an adult who loses the capacity to operate it, so that the money can be used to meet the adult's daily living expenses.
- Changing the law to solve the problems that arise when many banks freeze the funds in a joint account if one of the holders loses capacity.
- Giving those responsible for medical treatment a general authority to treat adult patients who are unable to give their consent. Relatives will have to be consulted and certain treatments will not be covered by this general authority.
- Sheriff Courts will be able to make one-off orders to deal with specific decisions faced by adults with incapacity such as selling a house or signing an important document.
- Creating a new office with the court system called the Public Guardian whose functions will include keeping public registers of attorneys, intervention orders and guardians and supervising those with financial powers.

During the parliamentary stages of the bill, a considerable amount of attention was paid to Part 5, which concerned consents for medical treatment, and in particular that some of its provisions would permit euthanasia 'by the back door'. In the course of the debates on the bill, assurances were given by the Scottish Executive that the legislation would not permit euthanasia and that a balance had been struck between the opinions of the proxy (the person who looks after the adult with incapacity) and the doctor who treats the adult with incapacity.

# MENTAL HEALTH (PUBLIC SAFETY AND APPEALS) (SCOTLAND) ACT, 1999

This was the first piece of legislation passed by the Scottish Parliament, and it was made necessary because of the release of Noel Ruddle from the State Hospital at Carstairs on the basis of a loophole in the law. The legislation added public safety to the grounds for not discharging certain patients detained under the Mental Health (Scotland) Act 1984 and provided a right of appeal against a sheriff's decision on applications for the discharge of such patients.

# PRIVATE MEMBERS' LEGISLATION

A private members' bill which, if passed, will have a significant effect on the Scottish legal system, is the Abolition of Poindings and Warrant Sales Bill, promoted by Tommy Sheridan, MSP (Scottish Socialist Party, Glasgow). The proposed legislation, which is expected to be implemented in the next year, will abolish what is commonly regarded as the most archaic and inhumane aspects of Scots law of diligence (the law relating to the collection of unpaid debts). After opposing the bill to Stage 1, the Scottish Executive had to accept defeat in the face of a report from three Scottish Parliament Committees which recommended that the bill be approved in principle. The Scottish Executive's opposition had been based on a concern that there would need to be an alternative method of diligence available to ensure the continued enforceability of debts. The bill's implementation will be delayed to allow the Scottish Executive to come up with such an alternative.

In the meantime, Alex Neil, the SNP list MSP for Central Scotland, lodged another proposal for a members' bill, the Bank Arrestment (Scotland) Bill which will make a minor but significant change to the law relating to the arrestment of bank accounts.

# HUMAN RIGHTS

When the Scotland Act 1998 was passed, the European Convention of Human Rights was incorporated into Scots law. This means that any legislation enacted by the Scottish Parliament may not include provisions which are incompatible with Convention rights, nor can the Scottish Executive perform any act which would be contrary to the provisions of the Convention. Any such legislation or act of the Scottish Executive can be challenged in Scottish courts and tribunals and effectively disapplied. Scotland is the first part of the UK to apply any part of the Human Rights Act 1998 which comes into force in its entirety throughout the UK on October 2nd 2000.

As far as the criminal law is concerned, this incorporation means that the actings of the Lord Advocate, Scotland's chief prosecutor, have been open to challenge since the Lord Advocate became a member of the Scottish Executive on May 20th 1999.

It is probably fair to say that the wide-ranging implications of the incorporation of the European Convention on Human Rights into Scots law had not been appreciated until it actually happened. In the year since the Scottish Parliament was established, a number of challenges have been made on the basis of Convention rights, including the Lord Advocate's appointment of temporary sheriffs which was deemed to be in breach of Article 6 of the Convention ('right to an independent and impartial tribunal'). Because Scottish temporary sheriffs had no security of tenure and depended on the Scottish Executive for their continued appointment, they were deemed to lack sufficient independence given that the Lord Advocate is a member of the Scottish Executive. The Scottish Executive has as a result published a draft Judicial Appointments etc (Scotland) Bill which is proposing abolition of the office of temporary sheriff. It has also recruited an additional nineteen permanent sheriffs since the temporary sheriffs were suspended.

Other issues which were challenged under the Convention included aspects of road traffic law covering the use of speed cameras; and the children's hearing system, Scotland's unique juvenile justice system.

# OTHER MATTERS

It would be irresponsible not to mention the fact that the Scottish Parliament was carefully scrutinised by the courts in its first year. The *Scotsman* newspaper took an action for judicial review at the end of September, during the so-called 'Lobbygate' affair because of a concern that the Standards Committee should not be meeting in private to consider the matter. The case was later dropped when the Standards Committee agreed not to discuss any matters of substance in private.

Also in the autumn of 1999, the Countryside Alliance supported a petition for interdict in the Court of Session in a bid to halt the progress of the Protection of Wild Mammals Bill, Mike Watson's private members' bill. The court action was an attempt to halt progress of the bill and lead to the Scottish Executive withholding its support for the bill.

The court action was brought by three people who claimed title and interest to sue because they alleged that their livelihoods would be affected by the bill. The petitioners claimed that Mike Watson had broken parliamentary rules during the preparation of his bill by accepting outside help in drafting the bill and the services of a researcher. The Parliament's Standards Committee had said at the time that the MSP had not broken the 'advocacy rule' as he had not received any cash or other benefits himself.

The action was rejected by Lord Johnson at the end of November 1999 when he said that the courts could not interfere with the workings of the Scottish Parliament. The appeal against this decision was dismissed on February 16th 2000. However, the court also ruled that the Scottish Parliament is not above the law, and that the courts have jurisdiction over the legislature, which unlike the Westminster Parliament, is a body created by statute, and therefore its powers are limited by statute. Lord Rodger said, 'It is a body which like any other statutory body must work within the scope of those powers. If it does not do so, then in an appropriate case the court may be asked to intervene and will require to do so' (Whaley et al, 2000).

## LOOKING FORWARD

The Scottish Parliament's first session runs until May 2003. In the period between now and then, a considerable amount of activity on the law reform side is planned. Already announced are further land reform measures, including a Land Reform Bill which will provide for the right to have responsible access to land for recreation and passage. The bill will also allow for the possibility of a community right to buy when property changes hands. Further planned land reform measures include reform of the law on title conditions, of the law of the tenement (which regulates rights and responsibilities of property with common parts, such as flatted developments) and of leasehold casualties.

Mental welfare law is currently under review by a committee being chaired by Bruce Millan, a former Secretary of State for Scotland, and the conclusions of the Lord MacLean's committee on the law relating to serious and violent sexual offenders will also require changes in the law in due course.

Further changes to the law of diligence will be considered by a group being set up by the Minister for Justice, and the Scottish Executive is committed to bringing forward legislation by 2001 to replace poindings and warrant sales. That, along with the conclusions from a review of charity law, changes to family law, and reform to the judicial appointments system, should ensure a very full land reform programme running well beyond the life of this Parliament.

# SECTION 3 beyond the mound: multi-layered governance

# CHAPTER 13: the executive and local government

## colin mair

In common with other chapters in this section, it will be impossible to examine the evolving nature of the relationship between the Executive and local government without commenting on what was inherited from the previous constitutional dispensation in the UK and Scotland. This inheritance includes an absence of formal constitutional protection for local government in the UK, a highly prescriptive framework of statute and guidance determining local government's powers to act, and the most centralised system of local government finance in Western Europe. As the report of the Commission on Local Government and the Scottish Parliament noted:

> *The arrival of the Scottish Parliament represents a fundamental change in the political landscape within which Scottish councils in the future will operate. Although Parliament and local government each have a democratic base, the Parliament will have the ultimate power of determining what becomes of local government.*
>
> **(Commission on Local Government, 1999: 11)**

While it is correct that Parliament has the ultimate power, the attitudes and behaviour of the Executive was clearly going to be a critical factor. The significant powers the Executive inherited with respect to local government, combined with the financial constraint it itself faced from the outset, (see below) meant that local government regarded it potentially as more a threat, than an opportunity. The McIntosh Commission Report expressed the matter in stark terms:

> *If local government does not deliver to the Parliament's satisfaction, Parliament will look elsewhere - perhaps to appointed bodies*

*accountable to Ministers. The change would probably not be sudden or rapid, but the trend would be inexorable.* (ibid, 1999: 13).

It is not possible here to cover all interactions between the Executive and local government that developed in the first year. For convenience we address three that cover the year chronologically, and may be seen as emblematic of the developing relationship: the treatment of the McIntosh Commission Report, the 2000/2001 financial settlement for local government, and the arrangements for the next Comprehensive Spending Review that will determine public service plans, priorities and spending targets for Scotland for the next three years. We review these in turn below after examining the inherited framework of central-local relations that sets their context.

One final introductory point will be useful. It is a truism that participants' beliefs, attitudes and expectations are a key part of relationships and how they develop. In the present context, participants' prior beliefs about what the relationship between government and local government should be are important, as is the degree to which these prior beliefs have been modified by experience. A key contention of this chapter is that important movement has taken place in the understanding of the relationship between Executive and local government across the year. Such a change has itself transformational potential.

# THE INHERITANCE

The Parliament inherited a framework for local government in Scotland that was highly centralised by European standards. As local government is a wholly devolved function, central powers previously held by Westminster simply passed over to the Parliament, and the Executive. They would now decide how many councils there are in Scotland, what their powers and functions should be, how they will be financed and how much they can spend. Furthermore, the existence of an elected Parliament and elected local government without explicit constitutional differentiation and protection raised the issue of managing dual and possibly contradictory mandates where the Parliament holds all the legislative power.

The focal point that expressed much of the concerns here is the financing of councils. As a consequence of reforms under Conservative governments, local government in Scotland raised directly under 20 per cent of its own income through Council Tax, with the vast bulk of income coming from central grants and business rate income determined and distributed by government.

Furthermore, a guidelines and capping system had evolved that empowered the Secretary of State to limit the level of expenditure proposed by councils in their budgets. This combination of government directly controlling over 80 per cent of council income, and having the power to limit how much was raised locally is viewed by local government as obscuring accountability. For example, if a council was forced to make cuts because of a reduction in central grants, who was politically responsible? The government, the council who decided what cuts should be made or both?

This situation is made worse by the Parliament's own financial basis. The vast bulk of the Parliament's spending is funded by block grant from Westminster subject to a Departmental Expenditure Limit; that is, a cash limit. This is increased over time by the Barnett Formula, which gives Scotland a share of UK public spending growth-based pro rata on its share of the UK population. As Scotland's population share is relatively declining, then the Parliament has in-built pressure on its core budget.

Public spending in Scotland other than that financed by Westminster grant is defined by the Treasury as devolved self-financed expenditure. This currently consists of that part of council spending which is financed by Council Tax and business rates raised in Scotland (taken together about £2.8bn per annum). Although local government finance is a devolved matter, these taxes are caught up in the Treasury's UK-wide control framework. A 1999 Treasury paper on the financial arrangements for devolution states that if Council Tax increases more rapidly in Scotland than in England and, as a consequence, the Treasury has to pay out proportionally more in Council Tax rebate to Scotland than England, then the block grant to the Parliament will be cut in compensation (HM Treasury, 1999).

More generally, the paper also states that:

*It is, however, open to the United Kingdom government to take into account levels of this self-financed expenditure in each country when determining the devolved budget where:*

- *Levels of self-financed spending have grown significantly more rapidly than equivalent spending in England over a period; and*
- *This growth is such as to threaten targets set for the public*

*finances as part of the management of the United Kingdom economy.* **(HM Treasury, 1999)**

The upshot is that, if the Parliament fails to control increases in Council Tax and business rates to a level broadly in line with English increases, its grant from Westminster may be penalised accordingly.

The final legacy the new system inherited was a distinctive understanding of central-local government relations. That they are separate - constitutionally and institutionally - led to a strong view on the local government side that legal, financial and administrative arrangements should ensure that they have distinctive decision-making spheres, and accountabilities. For example, the recurrent call for a review of local government finance has typically been predicated on demonstrating that the current financial arrangements do not stack up well against this normative model. They restrict local decision-making rights and as a consequence compromise clean accountability by councils to the communities that elect them. The reforms typically proposed - reduced central government financial contributions, a broader and more buoyant local tax base, and the elimination of capping - are all intended to liberate local decision-making and focus accountability. Given the constraints noted above, this was always going to be a source of tension.

# THE COMMISSION ON LOCAL GOVERNMENT AND THE PARLIAMENT

Notwithstanding, the Commission title, in fact it was asked to address two questions not one. The first concerned how effective relations could be built between Parliament, the Executive and councils; the second concerned how councils can best make themselves responsive and accountable to the communities that they serve (Commission on Local Government, 1999). The report ties the two questions together. If councils wish respect and parity of esteem in their relationship with Parliament and Ministers then they have to accept reform and development that would improve the inclusiveness and transparency of local political decision-making, the efficiency and effectiveness of services, and the scrutiny of performance. In short, they must embrace 'modernisation'. Equally, however, if Parliament and Ministers want an effective and accountable system of local government, they must be willing to create the context in which that is possible, and to enter into a real relationship with councils. Rightly, the Commission argued that their recommendations were an integrated package from which there could be no cherry picking.

The Executive's response in September 1999 was positive and, with two critical exceptions, the recommendations were accepted. The recommendations for reviewing and reforming local government were all accepted. The recommendation that councils review their political decision-making process to improve transparency, scrutiny, inclusiveness and efficiency has been progressed, and councils are currently engaged in this review. In particular, they have been asked to consider Executive/Cabinet systems of decision-making. Recommendations concerning the creation of proportional representation elections for local government, the remuneration of local members, and the electoral cycle are being progressed by the Renewing Local Democracy Group, chaired by Richard Kerley and due to report in June 2000.

Major recommendations concerning the relations between Parliament, Executive and local government were also endorsed. The recommendation that Parliament and councils enter into a Covenant setting out the basis for their working relationship has progressed to a draft document, although it is largely rhetorical rather than practical. However, it has been linked to the Commission's recommendation that a standing Joint Conference be established, and that Joint Conference will be able to monitor, review and renew the Covenant and its implementation over time.

The recommendation that councils and Ministers establish a working agreement has also progressed to draft form, and the draft includes the right of local government to be consulted on all relevant matters, involvement in pre-legislative scrutiny and the facility for local government to propose new legislation or amendments to existing legislation.

The crunch for local government, however, were the two key recommendations that implied modifying the financial and legal framework in which councils operate to create greater empowerment and accountability. The Commission proposed an independent review of local government finance as critical to promoting democratic local accountability and responsiveness. In particular, they saw a system where Parliament controls over 80 per cent of local income and retains the power to cap council spending as incompatible with strong local democracy. The Executive rejected this recommendation. Second, the Commission recommended that councils be given a power of 'general competence' to act flexibly and responsively in the interests of their communities, rather than being limited by statute as at present. In effect, the Executive should give up the power to determine the precise basis on which councils can act, and spend, on behalf of their communities. The Executive indicated it did not think that such a power of general competence was necessary but adopted the holding mechanism of a consultation exercise rather than outright rejection of the recommendation.

This treatment of the Commission's recommendations was a defining moment in the relationship between the Executive and councils. Recommendations reforming local government were wholly accepted, recommendations about covenants and working agreements were endorsed and progressed, but substantive recommendations that would have potentially limited the Executive's control over local government were either rejected or deferred. It did not fit well with rhetoric of trust and respect, and equal partnership. Legal and financial controls were being kept in place, presumably for use.

## THE 2000/2001 FINANCIAL SETTLEMENT

Such a reading of the Executive's intentions for local government was reinforced by the 2000/2001 financial settlement. The headline increase in grant aided expenditure (GAE), the level of spending by councils that the Executive deems acceptable, was 3.4 per cent (£193.8m). The bulk of that increase was ring fenced or earmarked for new service developments determined by the Executive, not councils; that is, hypothecated and not open to local choice.

The hypothecated increase relates largely to developments in education. The very public announcement of the headline figure by the Executive created public expectations of growth, but against inflation of around 3 per cent, councils were always going to have to make cuts in services other than those prioritised by the Executive through hypothecation. Councils resent hypothecation as it, in effect, determines councils priorities for them, rather than allowing them to make their own decisions within the totals available to them.

As well as hypothecation, the proportion of local spending the Executive proposed to fund through grant and business rate declined, continuing the trend from the last year of the previous Conservative government to the present.

While re-balancing the central and local contribution to local spending to promote greater local accountability may be desirable, if councils have only a single, non-buoyant tax source available to them (Council Tax), reductions in the Executive's contribution produce sharp increases in local tax levels. This year, the effect was that many councils were obliged to announce simultaneously council tax increases above the level of inflation and service cuts.

Understandably, this situation has led many in local government to conclude that the Executive is into 'business as usual', reviving calls for an independent review of local government finance, as recommended by the Commission.

# THE COMPREHENSIVE SPENDING REVIEW (CSR)

The CSR is a device by government to review, and project its policies, priorities and spending plans across a three-year period and in the light of economic forecasts and projections of fiscal receipts and public borrowing. In essence, it is a three-year strategic and financial plan for UK public services. The process is intended to ensure prioritisation within and between public expenditure programmes. The Scottish Office participated in the first review in 1998 as a department of the UK government. The Scottish Executive and Ministers will participate in the current review round on behalf of the Parliament. Their participation will have two related concerns. First, to ensure that Scotland's share of available UK public spending is protected and, secondly, to determine priorities and three year spending plans for Scottish public spending programmes.

Local government has been included in this process. COSLA as the representative body of Scottish local government, and professional associations such as SOLACE, ACPOS, CIPFA, ADES, and ADSW, have worked jointly to produce representations as part of the Scottish spending review. At the outset for these bodies, the focus was on estimating demand and cost factors that would influence local government's spending requirements across the next three years and, in effect, to make a bid for an appropriate share of the Scottish public spending planned and controlled by the Parliament.

However, since the process began in January, all parties have agreed the need to develop mechanisms for joint planning and co-determination of priorities between Ministers and the political leadership of councils, and agreements that would relate funding and spending to clear performance expectations. The joint submission from SOLACE and the professional associations proposes joint planning and decision-making, including the development of Public Service Agreements (PSAs) between Ministers and council political leaderships covering priorities, performance expectations, and funding. COSLA has also endorsed the need for a more robust framework for joint planning and prioritisation, and three year stability in funding to allow councils to plan in a strategic way. The Finance

Minister has publicly endorsed three-year budgets focussed on agreed outcomes. This modest consensus seems largely technical in character and well short of a revolution in thinking. Furthermore, how quickly, and how far, it develops is as yet unknown.

The key point is that it begins to challenge the understanding of Executive-local government relations that has underpinned previous thinking, and to move beyond a conceptualisation of Scottish governance as based on two separate elected levels of government pursuing their own distinctive purposes in isolation. As noted, in the major areas of local spend (education, social work, police etc.), issues of national as well as local priorities, national as well as local expectations, mean that national and local objectives in isolation make little sense. These recent developments are closer to accepting that the Executive and local government are inextricably linked in policy making, financing and being accountable for core services, and the key issue is whether partnership arrangements for decision-making are sufficiently developed.

We need to move beyond crude imposition of priorities by the Executive, and the confused accountability that follows, but that will not be achieved by clinging to a view of what local government should be that is unrelated to the realities of its role and context. A more positive and transformational move is to develop real partnership in governance, decision-making and accountability.

## CONCLUSION

This first year has been dominated by the inheritance from the old system. The legal, financial and governance frameworks were all in place, as were attitudes established under the previous dispensation. The Executive's response to the McIntosh Commission and the management of the financial settlement have tended to express and reinforce these inherited attitudes. Indeed, a purely documentary focus on what has happened this year might well lead to the conclusion that nothing much changed at all.

The key development, and a positive one, has been the recent willingness at Executive and local government levels to re-examine and begin to rethink what the relationship could and should be. This development does not mean that tensions over priorities, funding and spending controls will vanish (in fact, they seem built into the constitutional and financial framework of devolution). However, the development of a framework for joint planning and decision-making would allow them to be addressed and negotiated more intelligently. If 'modernisation' is to be more than a ragbag of initiatives, it must be about a willingness to think in new ways about the governance of Scotland under devolution, and to develop ways of dealing with mutual responsibility and interdependence effectively.

# CHAPTER 14: relations with westminster

## catherine macleod

On April 7th 2000, in Cardiff, only ten months after the opening of the Scottish Parliament, the Prime Minister presided over for the first time the Joint Ministerial Committee (JMC). Health Ministers from Westminster, Scotland, Wales and Northern Ireland met on an equal political footing to share and exchange ideas on best practice in health related matters. The symbolic importance, to demonstrate trust and confidence on all sides, cannot be exaggerated. The Scottish and Welsh Ministers did not expect to be told what to do, were not told what to do, and were there with the same degree of authority and credibility as their Whitehall counterparts.

The JMC's role, imaginatively extended by Gordon Brown to a forum for co-operation as well as problem-solving, will be tested in future years, if and when tensions and conflicts arise between and among Westminster departments and the devolved authorities. But their very existence, fostering familiarity and an element of trust between Ministers in every department in Edinburgh and London, in private at least, will encourage co-operation, diminishing the need for problem solving.

## THE FIRST STAGE OF A NEW RELATIONSHIP

Relations between Westminster and the Scottish Parliament are still very much in the evolutionary stage but so far the signs in Westminster augur well for the future. Westminster politicians want the Scottish Parliament to work. They believe that, with a positive response from Scotland, partnership should be possible. That Tony Blair and Gordon Brown, the two most important politicians in the land, have a vested interest in the success of devolution, and the determination and influence to assist its passage, is probably the relationship's defining factor.

The Prime Minister and Donald Dewar, Scotland's First Minister, recognised immediately the Holyrood votes were counted, that coalition government in Scotland would inevitably lead to a change in emphasis, different conclusions reached on either side of the border. From the outset, Tony Blair recognised the Scottish Executive would make its own decisions.

Contrary to popular belief, Downing Street has never tried to instruct Scotland's First Minister. It has offered advice but whether it is taken, or not, is entirely the prerogative of the Scottish Executive. Over the reform of Section 28, Downing Street's advice had no effect on the Scottish agenda but their intervention in the row over the lifting of the ban on beef on the bone, another devolved issue, curtailed the potential for conflict. Rather than the Scots or Welsh taking unilateral action, they were persuaded to work on a coherent UK approach with the Ministry of Agriculture and Fisheries in Whitehall.

The lack of public censure in London over the political fallout from Section 28 illustrated how indulgent Westminster politicians were prepared to be. The furore in Scotland unhelpfully turned the spotlight on the progress of the controversial legislation at Westminster yet UK Ministers lent only undiminished support to their Scottish colleagues. Westminster noted it was left to Tony Blair, on a visit to Scotland, to lead a head-on challenge to the critics of the Scottish Executive's proposals.

The Cubie proposals on student finance had the potential to generate real division between Westminster and Scotland as they spelt the end of a uniform system of student funding throughout the United Kingdom. At the end of the day, after David Blunkett, Westminster's Secretary of State for Education, had his say, the expected heavy hand of Downing Street failed to materialise. The wellbeing of the settled government of Scotland took precedence over the political will of the policy's critics.

Now, with Cubie behind them, there is every expectation in Westminster that the Labour/Liberal Democrat coalition will hold until the next Scottish Parliamentary election, a hugely significant factor in the joint co-operation between the two parties at Westminster.

Increasingly, after the Liberal Democrats sensational by-election success at Romsey on May 4th 2000, the party leader, Charles Kennedy, will play a pivotal role in Westminster's relationship with Holyrood. While the party's Deputy Leader, Jim Wallace, becomes increasingly remote from Westminster, it will be his leader in London who maintains the bridges with Downing Street.

# PERSONAL POLITICS AND CHEMISTRIES

The level of trust between Downing Street - Nos. 10 and 11 - and Scotland's First Minister, and other members of the Scottish Executive is 'quite high', helped considerably by long established relationships. The influential role played by Pat McFadden, the Prime Minister's Scottish deputy chief-of-staff, and once Mr Dewar's researcher, cannot be overstated. Sitting at the heart of Downing Street, enjoying cross-party respect, a discreet sounding board, and an expert on constitutional reform, McFadden's awareness of the political sensitivities running through the government makes him an ideal interface between the two Parliaments.

Downing Street Chief of Staff, Jonathan Powell and chief policy adviser David Miliband, have played an important role, maintaining open lines of communication between the First Minister and other members of the Scottish Executive. In turn they have encouraged other Whitehall officials to co-operate with their counterparts in Scotland.

For the Prime Minister Scottish devolution is a box ticked - Westminster has delivered it - the Scottish politicians have to get on and make it work. It is almost as simple as that. Scottish charges of 'control freakery' miss the mark. Tony Blair understands the theory and the practice of parliamentary devolution. His difficulties have arisen mainly from his reluctance to relinquish his iron grip on the Labour Party and to devolve responsibility to its members for fear of returning to the party vagaries of the 1980s. But, after the debacles in London and Wales, and the residual resentment in Scotland over the initial MSP selection process, the party machine has accepted the need to re-establish trust with its disillusioned party members. Future ballots for devolved bodies will be conducted by one-member, one-vote.

In the Treasury, Chancellor Gordon Brown, a life long champion of devolution, and a Scot representing a Scottish constituency, pulls the levers to make devolution work. Since taking charge of Labour's election campaign for the Scottish Parliament in Spring 1999, little has emerged from the Treasury without cognisance of its impact on Scotland. And as long as Brown continues at the Treasury, the Barnett Formula, the source of increasing resentment amongst a tranche of English MPs, will remain unchanged. Like the Prime Minister, who believes a system that has worked well for 20 years need not be changed, Brown will refuse any entreaties for change from Ken Livingstone, London's first directly elected Mayor.

Beyond the Treasury, co-operation between individual Whitehall departments and St Andrew's House is mixed but mostly good, if still maturing. Officials in Scotland and London believe progress is stymied by the lack of political direction in Scotland. Four overarching Concordats underpin the framework for co-operation and communication between the Parliament. Civil servants in every department are encouraged to think of the impact any legislation may have on Scotland, as they already do in some departments in relation to European rules.

The extent of the co-operation is already astonishing. The Lord Chancellor, Lord Irvine of Lairg and Home Secretary Jack Straw, never the greatest advocates of devolution, both closely and enthusiastically co-operate with Scotland's Justice Minister, Jim Wallace. The Foreign and Commonwealth Office has encouraged the Scottish Parliament to forge independent relationships within the European Union, and advocated the building of bridges between the Scottish Parliament and candidate states for two fold reasons. Not only do the Foreign Office believe closer relations between Scotland and Europe will enhance the role and reputation of the Scottish Parliament, they also believe it will strengthen Britain's role and influence in Europe.

Seasoned Whitehall observers smile with incredulity at the evident co-operation between Agriculture Secretary, Nick Brown, a hostile opponent of devolution, and the Scottish Agriculture Minister Ross Finnie. In other Whitehall departments the extent of co-operation is not so well developed. Offers to co-operate on environmental issues were firmly rebuffed in Scotland. An invitation to join the committee with the remit to police the green credentials of every decision in Government was turned down, a decision that surprised the Whitehall machine, anxious to acknowledge that environmental concerns did not recognise borders.

In Culture, Media and Sport there is still the tendency to forget about the Scottish dimension. Decisions are still being made without enough reference to Scotland but the politicians blame 'untidiness' rather than 'territorialism'. Nowhere in Whitehall is the lack of co-operation suspected of being either intentional or malicious, and with greater confidence in Scotland, and greater awareness of the Scottish dimension in Whitehall, Ministers, north and south of the border, believe the teething difficulties can be overcome.

# NEW DIFFICULTIES

Ironically it is the relationship between the Scotland Office and the Scottish Parliament that is the most uneasily defined. While the Scotland Office will, as widely desired by the Scottish Executive, wither on the vine after the General Election, Whitehall veterans claim they are staggered at the lengths to which the Scottish Executive, and their officials, will go to exclude their Scottish colleagues, throughout Whitehall, but particularly in the Scotland Office.

Mr Dewar's reluctance to trust the Scots at Westminster is attributed to a paramount loyalty to the institution of the Scottish Parliament, irrespective of its political colour. Scottish MPs fume at the First Minister's refusal to refer to a Labour-led Scottish Executive.

The relationship between the Scottish Executive and Scotland's Westminster MPs is the most fractious. Relationships between individual MPs and MSPs flourish but MPs bitterly resent the disdain in which they are held by the Scottish Executive. Pro-devolution MPs, loyal to the party leadership, recite a litany of complaints at the manner in which the Scottish Labour leadership at Holyrood has cast them adrift.

Perhaps the most glaring example of the Scottish Executive's inability to recognise or acknowledge publicly the partnership on offer from Westminster's politicians took place in April 2000 at a press conference in Edinburgh. Motorola were taking over the disused Hyundai factory in Fife, in the biggest ever inward investment scheme in Scotland worth £1.6 billion pounds. One thousand potential jobs were an immediate likelihood, with the possibility of another 2,000 in the pipeline. Credit for the scheme should have gone to the Chancellor, without whose early and continuing support it would not have happened. Other Whitehall departments did what they could to deliver the investment. Not a mention of Gordon Brown's contribution was made by the Scottish Executive members at the press conference. But more remarkably, there was no room on the platform for Mr Brown who was relegated to a seat amongst the press corps. The Scottish Executive claimed the announcement for their own, and the Chancellor was left to wonder if his erstwhile Westminster colleagues believed they were running an independent Scotland.

It is the inability of the Scottish Executive to nurture, and acknowledge a partnership between Scotland and Westminster that generates most exasperation, and worry in Westminster. Donald Dewar is personally blamed for lacking leadership qualities, or even the political vision or interest to deliver a Labour agenda in Scotland. Increasingly Westminster Scots believe Scotland's First Minister is trying to run 'his own mini state'.

Others fear 'rampant paranoia' within Labour's ranks in Scotland causes Labour politicians at Holyrood to try to 'out-nationalise the nationalists'. Labour MPs at Westminster worry how little difference there is between the twenty and thirty somethings on the Labour and SNP benches, whose views seem virtually interchangeable. What Westminster MPs, mainly the Scots, find intriguing, not to say infuriating, is absence of reciprocated loyalty from Members of the Scottish Parliament. They claim the inclination of MSPs is still to pass the buck down south when it suits them, and to talk disparagingly of their colleagues in the south, rather than to present a united front.

Westminster MPs bitterly resented criticism north of the border over the decision to convene the Scottish Grand Committee. With important responsibilities reserved at Westminster - the economy, welfare reform, the New Deal, defence matters, for example - they were staggered by suggestions that the Scottish MPs should not scrutinise their impact on Scotland. Westminster's Ministers throughout the government remain determined to maintain a forum to consider political sensitivities around issues like Scottish shipbuilding. They will risk irritating their Scottish colleagues if they consider the issues too important to ignore.

While the SNP anticipate a Scotland that is much more autonomous than at present they too have accepted the need to maintain effective representation at Westminster. Margaret Ewing, who maintains a dual mandate at Westminster and Holyrood, acknowledged the SNP still had a 'job of work to do' at Westminster. Even the party's younger members are flocking to win nominations for Westminster at the next General Election. This may reflect a increasing acceptance within the SNP of the 'post-nationalism' of the former leader of the Welsh leader, Dafydd Ellis-Thomas, now in the Lords, who believes the idea of the 19th century nation state is dead and should be replaced by other, more imaginative solutions.

Only one year into the life of the Scottish Parliament it is difficult to predict how its relations with Westminster will evolve. There are too many imponderables. If there is the political will in the Scottish Parliament for an expansion of its powers, the relationship will be severely tested. If there is a non-Labour administration, processing legislative provisions opposed to one another, in either the Scottish Parliament or Westminster, co-operation might founder. When the personalities in power change the sense of separateness may become more pronounced. Uncharted waters maybe but the inevitable evolution of devolution.

If Labour wins the next general election at Westminster, the drive for a stable, entrenched partnership with Scotland's Parliament will continue. In the labyrinthine maze of Whitehall intricate networks will exist to bind the two Parliaments together long after the second Scottish parliamentary elections in 2003. Even if the political landscape changes these structures will take time to unravel.

devolution settlement in Northern Ireland have meant that there has been little opportunity so far for the arrangements to work effectively.

## SIGNIFICANT DEVELOPMENTS

Prior to devolution, European policy was developed in the context of UK government departments, including the Scottish Office. Post-devolution, these arrangements have had to be externalised and reorganised. European policy is developed between departments within the UK government and departments within the Scottish and other devolved administrations. Arrangements have been put in place governing the flow of information and setting up channels of communication. The basis of these arrangements is the Memorandum of Understanding published in October 1999. The Memorandum of Understanding is a political agreement drawn up between the UK government and the Scottish Ministers setting out the five basic principles underlying their relationship:

• the principle of good communication
• the principle of co-operation
• the principle of exchange of information
• the principle of confidentiality
• the principle of accountability (Memorandum of Understanding, 1999).

These principles are designed to ensure that lines of government remain open even after devolution. Both officials and Ministers are committed to co-operation. A Joint Ministerial Committee is set up, as is a committee of officials in which difficulties can be discussed and ironed-out. Similar arrangements were agreed between the UK government and the administrations in Belfast and Cardiff although the suspension of the Northern Ireland Executive delayed the full operation of these institutional arrangements.

These institutional arrangements have been specifically adapted to deal with European policy. The Joint Ministerial Committee can meet in a variety of functional formats, one of which is the European Union Joint Ministerial Committee chaired by the UK Foreign Minister. In this case, however, it is planned that the bulk of the work will be done by letter rather than in formal meetings.

In practice it seems that European policy issues are dealt with more as a matter of routine rather than through these grand arrangements. Indeed, given that the Council of Ministers itself meets in functional format, it would not always be appropriate for meetings to take place under the aegis of the Foreign Office. Problems of sheep and cattle farmers have been dealt with, for example, in bilateral and trilateral meetings between the relevant Scottish, Welsh and UK Ministers of Agriculture with the UK Minister negotiating the resultant agreed line in Europe. On a couple of occasions a Scottish Minister has participated in Council of Ministers meetings. Sarah Boyack, for example as Scottish Minister for Transport and the Environment, has participated in the Environment Council. It seems, however, that it has not been easy to arrange such participation in other contexts. As a rule, UK Ministers have been the main protagonists at the European decision making level. At the present state of devolution this principal role is inevitable. European legal rules require that the Minister voting in the Council has the power to bind the Member State as a whole. Without formal arrangements being in place to agree a mandate for a 'regional' Minister, a UK Minister is the only person having such full powers.

The development of a mandate for a regional Minister to act on behalf of all parts of the UK is not impossible in legal or constitutional terms, but is unthinkable in political terms until such time as the devolved institutions have begun to function permanently in Northern Ireland. When the devolved institutions were suspended, so too were the inter-governmental arrangements for co-ordination of policy set up under the Belfast Agreement. The North-South Ministerial Council and the British-Irish Council both have as part of their remit the exchange of information on European Union policy and discussion of implementation of European policy. The Scottish Executive is involved in the latter.

The Memorandum of Understanding and the subsequent Concordat on co-ordination of European policy issues that lays down the ground rules for co-operation between departments were negotiated at ministerial and departmental level. Much of the debate in the Scottish Parliament when they were presented to Parliament in October 1999 centred on the lack of accountability of the arrangements. Alex Neil, SNP list MSP for Central Scotland, for example, questioned how Parliament could scrutinise the work of the Joint Ministerial Council when minutes of its meetings were not to be made available and Ministers from all sides were bound by principles of confidentiality. Similar issues were raised in the Welsh Assembly when the Welsh version was debated. Ron Davies was particularly critical of the handling of European business arguing that Ministers from the devolved institutions could disagree with the UK line but would always be over-ridden by the UK Minister who would take the final decision. The UK Minister, of course, is not accountable to the devolved parliamentary bodies. The effect of these arrangements is therefore to strengthen the Executive as against Parliament.

This is not to say that the Scottish Parliament does not have a way into the policy making process. In its first year of operation, the European Committee of the Scottish Parliament embarked on a consultation process on its own work programme. In its report Forward Work Programme for January 2000 to June 2001, the committee stated that it would adopt an advocacy role on European matters. In particular it would 'pro-actively debate and discuss wider issues that are shaping the agenda in the European Union - with the committee acting both as a forum and a catalyst for debate' (European Committee, 2000: no page number). This role is in addition to one of scrutiny of European Union legislation and Scottish legislation implementing European obligations and responding to issues raised by the Scottish Executive on European policy developments. As part of its advocacy role, the European Committee recognised the need to formulate its own views at an early stage in order to influence Scottish Ministers but also directly to influence the European Commission. An early example of the success of this approach is the European Committee's (2000) 4th Report 2000 on mainstreaming environmental issues into government policy in Scotland. This report is a response to the European Commission's 6th Environmental Action Programme. Environmental policy is of course a devolved matter and it is both logical and desirable that an examination of the Commission's programme should be undertaken within the Scottish Parliament. It is also essential that Scottish and UK Ministers are at least aware of the views of the Parliament on such matters before they embark on any negotiations either at the level of the Joint Ministerial Council or at the level of the Council of Ministers.

It is probably fair to say that the European Committee in this first year has not developed this advocacy role to the extent that its members might have wished. As with all the other committees, the European Committee has been on a steep learning curve and has had to learn to deal with difficult questions of procedure - a point emphasised by Peter Lynch in his contribution (see Chapter Eight). It has also had to determine its own priorities whilst dealing with very difficult problems relating to structural funds that had arisen before the creation of the Parliament. At times the members of the committee have been inundated with paperwork and the committee gave the appearance of merely moving one set of papers from one desk to another. However, the forward work programme indicates that the committee has settled on certain manageable and selective tasks rather than attempting to deal with each issue that comes out of Europe.

# FUTURE DEVELOPMENTS: SCOTLAND 2020

Two major developments will impact on Scotland's relations with Europe in the next few years. The most obvious of these is in relation to the enlargement of the European Union to absorb the countries of Eastern Europe. If Scotland is a peripheral nation now within the European Union, its peripherality will be further demonstrated by an eastern expansion to take in countries such as Poland, Hungary and Slovenia in the relatively near future. Scotland then needs to determine its strategic allies.

One effect of enlargement, however, is likely to be a weakening of centralised policy making with European level decisions becoming much more flexible and open-ended. If this is the case, the Scottish Parliament and Executive will be given greater discretion on how European policy is adapted to Scottish needs. In the area of the environment, for example, Scotland may decide to loosen regulatory controls and sacrifice environmental concerns to permit rapid industrial development choosing a minimalist interpretation of future European legislation. Alternatively, Scottish priorities could be set in terms of strict environmental controls and sustainability. Enlargement will inevitably lead to greater autonomy of all parts of the European Union as centralised control will become unwieldy and counter-productive. Scotland will therefore be faced with more choice and more possibilities for action. Strategic planning for Scotland 2020 is therefore a priority. Where does Scotland want to be in 2020? What allies have we made? Where are our key relationships?

The second major development will turn on the outcome of the next round of world trade talks. These talks will themselves influence European Union policy on matters of agricultural trade, the shape of permissible regulatory controls, the limits of state or government intervention in the market. Free trade policies currently pursued within the European Union tempered with social and redistributive objectives may be displaced by a North American view of the benefits of liberal market policies. In this case, Scotland will have to adapt quickly to rapid shifts in demand and will need to determine strategies for competing in a very different world setting. Scottish policies will need to be set in terms of maximising the potential of each individual and concentrate on competitiveness and openness. There should at least be debate in Scotland about the effects of any shift in World Trade Organisation policy as part of the Scotland 2020 debate.

relations with the european union

# racism and the scottish parliament

## elinor kelly

In February 1999 the report of the Stephen Lawrence Inquiry was published In London. In March one man was brought to trial in Edinburgh accused of the murder of Surjit Singh Chhokar and there was widespread protest about how the trial was conducted. In May the Scottish Parliament was elected. In July, the Crown Office announced that there would be a second trial relating to the Chhokar murder. In August the new Justice Minister released his Action Plan for Scotland and formed a steering group. Starting work so soon after the Stephen Lawrence Inquiry, while the scandal of the Chhokar trial was at a peak, Jim Wallace, the Justice Minister, could have seized the moment and put racism firmly onto the agenda. Instead, work proceeded slowly. Part of the problem is that lawyers in Scotland have practised for many years without ethnic monitoring of criminal statistics, without any study of the racial incidents reported to the police, without a professional interpreting service and without community liaison, so radical change did not seem an imperative.

Then in February 2000, things began to change. The Equal Opportunities Committee insisted that Mr Wallace and his civil servants in the General Register Office introduce a question on religion into the 2001 Census for Scotland. In March, Cathy Jamieson, MSP, challenged the UK government about their measures on asylum and their refusal to allow Scotland any say in the arrangements that would apply to asylum-seekers sent north. The cocoon of complacency about Scotland's public affairs was starting to be unravelled by parliamentary debate and committee. At last, in April, the Solicitor-General issued new guidelines requiring the courts to ensure that those convicted for racism receive stronger sentences for their crimes, ending their longstanding tradition that they need not take racism seriously (even in murder trials such as the cases of Axmed Sheekh in 1989, Shamsudden Mahmood in 1994 and Imran Khan in 1998). Thus, the first year of the Scottish Parliament ended with decisive action by a law officer.

The Chhokar family, however, is still waiting for justice. Their son was killed in November 1998. The second trial has not started. Institutional racism remains intact in the Scottish justice system. Will the Scottish Parliament take it apart in its second year?

# CHAPTER 16: developments in quangoland

## jean mcfadden

## QUANGOS: THE SCALE OF THE PROBLEM

There are currently 186 quangos in Scotland which operate in areas devolved to the Scottish Parliament (Scottish Executive, 2000). The government prefers to call them public bodies. They can be broken down into six categories:

- Executive Non-Departmental Public Bodies (NDPBs)
- Advisory Non-Departmental Public Bodies
- Certain tribunals
- Nationalised Industries
- Public Corporations
- NHS Bodies

Total expenditure by the NDPBs amounts to around £2 billion per annum, while the expenditure by NHS bodies amounts to £4.5 billion per annum. The total of £6.5 billion is almost 50% of the expenditure under the Scottish Parliament's control. Individual quangos spend huge amounts of public money, is some cases more than some local authorities. Scottish Enterprise's budget in 1998-9 was £443.3 million, while that of Scottish Homes was £349 million. The responsibility for appointments to these public bodies now lies with the Scottish Ministers. Altogether they are responsible for almost 3,900 appointments to public bodies, almost three times the total number of elected members in Scotland. Some of these appointments attract considerable salaries. The chairman of the Scottish Environmental Protection Agency, for example, receives almost £40,000 per annum for a three day week (Scottish Executive, 2000)

## QUANGOS: JOBS FOR THE BOYS?

Quangos have long been a source of controversy, regardless of which political party is in power. The Conservatives, in opposition, accuse the Labour government of packing quangos with their own supporters to carry out their political agenda, just as Labour accused the Conservatives when they formed the government. The criticism of the Conservative government became particularly intense in Scotland in the 1990s as the Conservative Party lost electoral support both at Westminster and in local government. A further criticism was the formation of powerful new quangos, such as Scottish Homes and Scottish Enterprise which, to some extent, fulfil roles which had traditionally been carried out by local government. In addition, as a result of the Conservative government's controversial reorganisation of Scottish local government in 1995-6, several further local government functions, such as water and sewerage, were removed from local government and handed over to quangos.

## EXPECTATIONS OF THE SCOTTISH PARLIAMENT

One of the hopes of those who supported the establishment of a Scottish Parliament was that quangos in Scotland would come under more effective scrutiny and control and that some of their activities might be returned to an elected tier of government in Scotland. The Scottish Constitutional Convention, which developed the blue-print for the Scottish Parliament, expressed concern not only over the steady transfer of important areas of government from elected representatives to unelected and unrepresentative quangos but also over the key policy areas which quangos run including Scotland's hospitals, much of its housing provision, and whole swathes of the environment, cultural and economic development and educational provision (Scottish Constitutional Convention, 1995).

In 1997, a John Wheatley Centre report examined quangos in Scotland. It identified the following further areas of concern:

- The expenditure of quangos;
- The loss of public accountability in areas of policy where previously there was a measure of public accountability;
- Their methods of operation, often associated with secrecy, hostility to community concerns and excessive remuneration (John Wheatley Centre, 1997: 3-4).

Its main recommendations in terms of responsibilities were:

- In the case of the NHS, local government could take over responsibility for (not necessarily the direct provision of) primary, community and long stay services;

- Various functions of Scottish Homes should be transferred to the Scottish Executive and Scottish Parliament;
- The functions of local enterprise companies should be transferred in their entirety to local government while the training functions of Scottish Enterprise should be transferred to a department of the Scottish Executive (ibid: 14-20).

# A BONFIRE OF QUANGOS?

In opposition, the Labour Party promised a bonfire of quangos and the Chairmen of the Water and Sewerage Authorities were warned that they would be expected to clear their desks when a Labour government was elected. In government, the rhetoric was toned down considerably.

The White Paper, *Scotland's Parliament*, listed the public bodies which would come within the remit of the Scottish Parliament and made it clear that the Parliament would be able to investigate and monitor them, alter their structure, wind up existing bodies and create new ones (Scottish Office, 1997: para. 2.9). Although the government recognised that some executive functions of government are best delivered by public bodies, concern was expressed at the extent to which Scotland's vital public services are run by quangos (ibid: para. 6.7). Specifically, the Scottish Executive would be required to put arrangements in place to ensure that appointments to Scottish public bodies are subject to scrutiny and conform to the Code of Practice of the Commissioner for Public Bodies (ibid: para. 6.8).

# PROGRESS SO FAR

One year into the life of the Scottish Parliament, there are just as many quangos as on the day the Parliament was established. There has as yet been no transfer of any of the functions of quangos to local government, although the McIntosh Commission recommended that. Given the unique role of local government which stems from its elected status, in any review of other bodies delivering public services, the option of transfer to local government should always be considered. Likewise where new services are being developed prior consideration should always be given to whether local government should be the vehicle of delivery, subject to efficiency and cost-effectiveness (Commission on Local Government, 1999: para. 62).

However, there has been some progress. In December 1999, Wendy Alexander, the Minister for Communities, announced that the quango status of Scottish Homes would be ended and that it would be turned into an Executive Agency with its Chief Executive reporting directly to Scottish Ministers. The unelected board is to go, to be replaced by a Management Board with two or three non-executive directors operating within a framework set by Ministers. Most of the staff of Scottish Homes are expected to transfer to the agency, but those who work in policy development are likely to transfer to other parts of the Scottish Executive. The vehicle for this change of status of Scottish Homes is to be a Housing Bill expected later this year.

Changes in the appointment procedures have been introduced, with vacancies being advertised and an independent assessor taking part in the interviews. Application forms have been redesigned and job descriptions and person specifications are being developed. Codes of Practice on openness, accountability and conduct have been developed.

Presumably as an interim measure, more councillors have been appointed to various quangos, for example to the Water Authorities and to certain Advisory NDPBs, such as the Ancient Monuments Board for Scotland. This, however, does not really address the accountability issue as the councillors are elected to their respective local authorities, not to the quangos.

The Ethical Standards in Public Life etc (Scotland) Bill, which is expected to reach the statute book by the summer of 2000, will provide a model code of conduct for members of devolved public bodies, to be issued by Scottish Ministers. Every public body is to have a statutory duty to promote the observance by its members of the code and of high standards of conduct generally. A Standards Commission is to be established (a new quango). This will have the power to consider alleged breaches of the code and if the Commission concludes that there has been a contravention of the code the member involved may be censured, suspended from the public body for up to one year or removed from membership of the body and disqualified from membership for up to five years. It is possible that disqualification may be extended beyond the individual body whose code has been breached.

## THE CONSULTATION EXERCISE

In February 2000, the Scottish Executive issued a consultation paper on the public appointments system. The Scottish Executive consider the key objectives of the procedures for making public appointments are that they should:

- Enjoy public confidence through being fair, open and transparent;
- Be proportionate i.e. appropriate to the nature of the posts and the size and weight of their responsibilities;
- Provide clarity and structure with the roles and responsibilities of the posts being clearly stated;
- Secure quality outcomes by getting the right people in the right posts;
- Encourage a wider range of people to apply;
- Be accessible and informative to those considering putting their names forward and to those being considered for appointment (Scottish Executive, 2000).

Key issues on which views are sought include the targets for appointing more people from under-represented sections of society which have been inherited from the Scottish Office. These include increasing the proportion of women from the 1998 level of 47% to 50% by 2002, increasing the number of people from an ethnic minority background from 0.4% to 1.3%, and encouraging more disabled people to apply (ibid: Ch. 2).

Another key issue is the question of payment for public service. At present, some appointees are salaried, some receive an attendance allowance, some receive nothing other than travel and subsistence allowances. The Scottish Executive are keen to consider suggestions to improve the appointment process and strengthen the independent element. A further key issue is whether there should be a Scottish Commissioner for Public Appointments and, if so, who should be responsible for the appointment and what powers should a Commissioner have (ibid: Ch. 3).

The final issue raised in the consultation process is the role of the Scottish Parliament. Should the Parliament have a pre-appointment involvement in nominations for appointment? How may post-appointment scrutiny by the Parliament be developed?

# EXPECTATIONS VERSUS REALITY

There may be some disappointment that there has not been more progress in the transfer of functions of Executive NDPBs to an elected tier of government. Part of the problem is that the Scottish Executive has not yet decided what it wants to do about local government. It would be premature to transfer functions to that level of government if it is to face another shake-up in the not too distant future. The Scottish Executive will also be wary of transferring too much to themselves lest they are accused of centralisation.

However, much has been done behind the scenes, including new interview procedures, to eliminate the charges of cronyism which surrounded previous appointments. The new codes of openness and accountability are forcing present quango chairs and members to re-examine their old methods of operation. The proposed legislation on an enforceable code of conduct should increase public confidence that any close connections between quango members and contractors or grant recipients will be declared and that failure to do so will be punished.

## FUTURE DIRECTIONS

A consultation paper is always gives a good idea of the way the Executive are thinking. It is quite clear that the Scottish Executive is determined to open up quango membership to an unprecedented extent and that the independent element in the appointment procedure will be strengthened. It is very likely that an independent Scottish Commissioner for Public Appointments will be appointed. The somewhat chaotic system of remuneration will be tackled with something more acceptable, intelligible and consistent put in its place.

There will undoubtedly be an increased role for the Scottish Parliament, although this is unlikely to extend to the confrontational confirmation hearings found in other countries. However, chairs of high profile quangos can expect to be grilled by the Parliament's committees.

But quangos are here to stay. A government needs specialist advisory bodies and tribunals, provided that the systems of appointment, payment and monitoring are transparent and robust. However, it is to be hoped that more of the functions of the powerful, high-spending Executive quangos will come under the control of a directly elected body.

# SECTION 4   civic scotland, identities and the isles

# CHAPTER 17: beyond the blethering classes: consulting and involving wider society

lucy mcternan

For a number of years in Scotland there has been a groundswell of interest in changing not just the institutions and processes of politics, but its underpinning culture. There has been a much-vaunted desire for a 'new politics', which is more consensual, inclusive, and less distant from the very communities and citizens it is supposed to serve.

The establishment of the new Scottish Parliament has been seen by many people as a historical opportunity to break with the past. Many hoped it would be an opportunity to leave behind as unwanted baggage the impenetrable rules and conventions of Westminster through the ages, along with the 'sleaze' of politics of the recent past. The aim was for politics which is accessible, relevant, and ultimately more democratic.

The experience of the first year of the Parliament in light of this has been mixed: offering both cheer to the optimists and succour to the cynics. The question for the future is whether those efforts to change the exclusive culture that have been made in these early days of the new system can be entrenched, or will be swept aside by time and 'business as usual'.

## BACKGROUND

This desire for formal politics to be more open and participative was a key feature of the work of the Scottish Constitutional Convention during the early 1990s and of the cross-party Consultative Steering Group, set up to consider the working practices of the Scottish Parliament following the positive referendum result in 1997 (Scottish Constitutional Convention, 1995; Consultative Steering Group, 1999).

It stems from a belief that wider social or 'civic' participation in government ensures greater relevance and creativity in policy-making and engenders good governance. It also comes against a backdrop of increasing popular disenchantment with politics, identifiable in falling political party membership and declining election turnouts.

Coming from the same stable of argument as the case for proportional representation, and indeed for devolution itself, it nevertheless goes a step beyond more conventional political debate, by admitting the existence and indeed desirability of a range of social, professional and voluntary networks beyond the formal 'political'. It can be seen either as a direct challenge, or as a complement, to the action of direct appeal by politicians (or others) to the public through effective use of print and broadcast media.

Engagement by aspects of the formal political process with civic bodies, it is argued, can lead to more detailed and informed debate, shared ownership of the direction of policy development, direct linkages to the communities affected, and therefore ultimately better decision-making. It was those very civic networks - church groups, trade unions and voluntary organisations - which nurtured and developed the case for devolution through the Constitutional Convention years.

The election of the Scottish Parliament by proportional representation, delivering closer political balance and necessitating coalition in government has arguably at a stroke moved Scotland closer to the ideal of 'new politics'. This is true to the extent that within political circles and institutions (across the UK) new rules are having to be learnt, but it falls short of reaching out to invite new players into the game. If politics in Scotland is to become consensual and participative in the way the concept of 'new politics' envisages, all the existing players have to make conscious and sustained efforts to alter their style, finding a level of engagement between populism and the politics of the inner circle.

The Consultative Steering Group recognised this explicitly, and the possible outstanding debt to Scottish civic society, in the third of the guiding principles of their report, stating that:

*the Scottish Parliament should be accessible, open, responsive, and develop procedures which make possible a participative approach to the development, consideration and scrutiny of policy and legislation.* **(Consultative Steering Group, 1999: 8)**

The problem with achieving this goal, however, is that it is not something the new Parliament can achieve by itself, nor by easily identifiable and tangible measures. By definition it requires action and change also in all the other aspects of the political system, including the Executive (Ministers and civil service), political parties, individual politicians, the media, civic society and the wider Scottish community. The 'access agenda' has remained elusive, the cause of many champions, and of none.

The CSG did make some practical procedural suggestions to further the agenda, including the use of petitioning and considering the co-option of non-MSPs on to committees. It also attempted to highlight areas for further debate, such as the definition and role of lobbyists.

It also recommended support for the establishment of a Civic Forum as a focus for (non-deliberative) debate outwith the Parliament, creative use of a range of consultation methods including new technology, and, more symbolically, that parliamentary committees should meet in different venues around the country.

The implementation, and success, or otherwise of these proposals provide some benchmarks to the progress of the access agenda so far, but of necessity a broader evaluation remains more subjective. What follows then, is a perspective from the voluntary sector, that dimension of modern Scottish society, which while actively involved in the delivery of public services, remains proudly independent of the state, and aware of its responsibilities to voice the interests of the communities it serves and involves. Voluntary organisations have been keen to get actively involved in the work of the Parliament, and to influence the programme and approach of the Executive. Largely unrecognised as stakeholders in policy-development in the past, our experience of the new Scottish system has been at once exciting and challenging, and predictable and disappointing, but nevertheless an interesting gauge of progress towards 'new politics'.

## THE PARLIAMENT

The Parliament's own efforts in its first year to develop into an accessible institution have on the whole been well-meaning, if tripped-up repeatedly by practical considerations such as time and resources. On the most concrete of levels - that of its physical presence - it has proved inaccessible to some individuals and groups. The Parliament's temporary home on the Mound is widely understood to be less than fit for purpose, and while controversy has raged about the plans and costs of the Holyrood site, representatives of key external bodies have failed to obtain seats in the smaller committee rooms at crucial meetings, and as anticipated disabled people have only partial access to the public spaces. Meeting space for members of the public, let alone resources such as desk space and ICT access are non-existent.

Nevertheless the Parliament Corporate Body has made welcome efforts to overcome the physical confines of the Mound. It has invested effectively in a user-friendly website reporting the business of the Parliament in a (usually) timely way. It has lent its co-operation and support to complementary initiatives such as the voluntary sector Parliamentary Information and Advice Service run by SCVO and the com.com/holyrood project which is providing ICT links to the Mound to community centres and village halls.

The committee clerks, while under pressure of time and endlessly competing demands, on the whole respond constructively to enquiries and suggestions. The committees themselves have been at pains to draw on the experiences of outside bodies in their preliminary investigations of issues, and the number and range of civic bodies that have been called to give evidence is impressive.

The Parliament has been more muddled in its approach to the less practical aspects of the 'access agenda'. The debates about the role of 'lobbyists', for instance, undertaken in committee were unhelpfully side-tracked by the early 'Lobbygate' scandal involving unsubstantiated allegations of privileged access to ministers of clients of a private lobby firm. Understandably parliamentarians wished to distance themselves and their new institution from the practices associated with the 'sleaze' scandals of previous years at Westminster, but the upshot was that far from seeking to identify ways of promoting the sensible participation of external bodies, the discussion focused on ways to exclude, such as a requirement for formal registration of all organisations approaching the Parliament. Inevitably it is a delicate distinction to make, but there is a clear difference between the activities of for-profit companies hired to influence parliamentary debate, and representatives of the myriad of voluntary organisations and community groups speaking directly on behalf of communities. Both have their place in the system, but the activities of one should not by implication limit the scope of the other.

Similarly the debate about the appropriateness of inviting non-MSPs to a formal role within committees has proved quite thorny, and is as yet unresolved. The Equal Opportunities Committee, rightly concerned at the lack of a perspective from minority ethnic communities amongst their own, elected, number, raised the prospect of co-opting an external member. Clearly this prompts significant questions about the exact role and responsibilities of such a person, and their representative mandate. The view was taken that 'full' co-opted committee membership was not legal, but that it was possible to appoint a 'standing advisor'. The Parliamentary Bureau and the Corporate Body are considering the issue.

Despite these debates, perhaps the most encouraging aspect to the Parliament's first year has been the evident enthusiasm of individual parliamentarians to engage with their communities. The open approach of most of the 129 has been received positively, and it is hoped will become an established cultural feature of the Parliament's work.

## THE EXECUTIVE

The Scottish Executive, perhaps because it is not operating from a 'blank sheet' in the same way as the Parliament has been slower to embrace the practicalities of open and participative government. It has committed itself to the *Modernising Government* programme initiated by the UK government, and there are some positive signs in the prevalent use of specialist 'commissions' and working groups designed to open up examination of policy issues beyond the ranks of the civil service. The early appointment of the Independent Committee of Inquiry into Student Funding (1999) may have been conceived as a political fix, but it developed into a good model of extensive consultation on a complex matter.

It will clearly take time and effort however for all branches of the establishment to become familiar with the range of options available to them to consult and encourage genuine participation, beyond the 'glossy document exercise' which many groups rightly regard with some cynicism. At the very least feedback as to the consideration, adoption, or otherwise of submissions to such exercises is much needed.

Cultural change of the type and to the degree required will not happen in the Scottish Executive and Non-Departmental Public Bodies overnight, and spells of disillusionment that it is all 'business as usual' have infected many over the course of the year. However the recent launch of an extensive information and consultation exercise by the Finance Minister on something as fundamental as the Executive's budget is certainly a welcome signal of intent.

# CIVIC SOCIETY

If the ambition of 'new politics' is to be realised to any extent in Scotland, responsibility also clearly lies with civic organisations and the public at large. Cynicism is perhaps the biggest danger to the whole process of change, and networking, sharing experiences, information, views and good practice can all help to engender and sustain a new style of engagement in public policy and decision-making. It is with this in mind that many in the voluntary sector have been strong advocates for the establishment of a Civic Forum to work alongside and complement the new Parliament.

The Executive has now committed some support to the establishment of a Civic Forum, the proposals for which grew out of the provisional work of the Scottish Civic Assembly grouping. Drawing together civic bodies including voluntary organisations, trade unions, churches, professional associations and business bodies, it is designed to provide an arena for discussion of pre-legislative proposals, whether Executive, Parliament or civic society generated.

Over 650 organisations across civic life and across Scotland registered their interest in the formation of the Civic Forum, and the level of interest in recent elections to its council suggest it will be a vibrant and pro-active body. It sees its locus in advising on and providing participation mechanisms, to ensure civic Scotland links with political Scotland more effectively.

Different elements of civic society, and through them the communities and individual Scots they involve, will continue to forge their own links with Executive and Parliament, but the Civic Forum will hopefully add a valuable dimension to this by encouraging the cross-fertilisation of ideas.

Of course the most effective way to open up public debate remains attracting the interest of the established media - print and broadcast. While the coverage of the July 1st opening of the new Parliament was overwhelmingly positive, the day to day reporting of politics under the new institutional arrangements has been slow to change, and remains largely negative in tone. Unfortunately, despite efforts to encourage journalists to broaden the analytical coverage of social issues, civic bodies continue to find it difficult to voice opinion on policy unless it can be interpreted as an attack on an individual politician or party.

# THE FUTURE

In many ways the 'access agenda' is the single most important challenge facing the new Scottish institutions. Nevertheless in reality simply keeping it as far up the list of political priorities as it should be over the crucial months and years to come will be hard work. Recent proposals by an ad hoc group of civic activists that a monitoring framework for participation should be set up jointly by Parliament, Executive and civic society (maybe a successor body to the CSG which originally set the agenda) have been discussed, but as yet nothing is in place. Until it is, it is incumbent on us all to continue to strive towards 'new politics'.

# CHAPTER 18: scottish business and the scottish parliament

## richard kerley

As the recently appointed Auditor General for Scotland has observed, our ancestors had some experience of business-government relations with the old Scottish Parliament. The creation of 'The Scottish Company' to trade in Darien, Panama was organised through a Parliamentary Act. It was a company virtually unregulated by any framework of financial responsibility or accountability, and its failure led to extensive financial disaster for many Scots, including many of the business and political elite. The collapse of the Darien venture and the financial consequences was therefore one central element in the agreement on The Act of Union between Scotland and England. (Black, 2000: 6). This unsuccessful business venture therefore had a dramatic and far-reaching impact on the economy, society and future of Scotland. In a curious historical reversal, a great deal of recent comment about the new Scottish Parliament implies or claims that it has the potential to have a disastrous impact on Scottish business.

This chapter assesses the powers and competencies that the Scottish Parliament has in relation to Scottish business and the initial reactions of business to the creation of the Parliament. It also considers some ways in which the Parliament can influence business decision making in a devolved Scotland and how business might seek to influence the Parliament.

## THE BACKGROUND

On the face of it claims of the potential disaster that the Parliament may wreak on business seem curious, particularly since the powers of the Parliament are largely confined to organisations and programmes in the public services. To all intents and purposes the new Parliament is actually a Parliament for the public services, and much of the debate in the first year has focused on public service impacts, particularly in education and health care.

Many of the key aspects of government action that have the greatest impact on business and the economy are reserved to the Westminster Parliament. Macro-economic policy, virtually all legislation related to employment, social security, and the fiscal and monetary system, and all those aspects of government, which maintain 'common markets for UK goods and services' will rest with Westminster (Scottish Office, 1997, para. 3.3).

Indeed, it is interesting to note that most of the complaints directed by business at government, most recently in relation to parental leave, energy taxes, and rights for part-time workers have actually been directed at the Westminster government (Taylor, 1999). So one question we need to consider in assessing the impact of the Scottish Parliament on business in Scotland is to ask just what was business so scared about? We can attempt to answer this question by examining relations between business and the Parliament in the first year of its existence, but first some background is necessary.

## BUSINESS AND THE BIRTH OF THE PARLIAMENT

Historically, most of the organisations representing business in Scotland have held views on devolution which ranged from lukewarm to hostile. In 1996 George Robertson, then Shadow Secretary of State, was described in one report as having had 'a difficult time persuading senior members of the Scottish business community that a Parliament would be to their advantage ' (Buxton, 1996).

The same article gave extensive space to the predominantly hostile or sceptical views of business organisations such as the Institute of Directors, the CBI and Scottish Financial Enterprise. Later in that year, Baur reported on a survey which established that such sentiments were held at the individual level as well. The annual *Insider* business elite study, carried out after Labour had launched its two question referendum strategy, showed 78 per cent of those questioned against a Parliament, and 77 per cent against it having tax raising powers if established. Concerns about the proposed Parliament appeared to have a number of different aspects; for some this was a political objection based on opposition to Labour and a fear that an elected body in Scotland would lead to 'permanent socialism' (Baur, 1996). For some there were concerns about Scottish based business alienating or becoming distanced from customers in England, with vague fears about an English 'backlash'. More widely expressed were fears about excess regulation and differential taxation.

In the period leading up to the publication of the White Paper, business concerns about differential taxation regimes were focused on corporate and business taxation (in the widest sense) where any change would have had particular significance for the financial services industries. Even the tax varying power on personal taxation became the focus of some critical or sceptical business comment in the run up to the referendum. Senior business executives such as the then Governor of the Bank of Scotland Sir Bruce Patullo commented on the undesirability of the Parliament having tax raising powers and he in turn became the subject of sustained and forceful public criticism by leading politicians.

Despite such business fears, as the prospect of the Parliament came ever closer, with the election of a Labour government, the referendum and Scotland Act, business generally appeared to set aside doubts and contribute some ideas about how the Parliament might work. Perhaps the most significant element of this was the array of expert working parties convened by Lord McDonald, collectively working to produce *Pathfinders to the Parliament: A Business Agenda for the Scottish Parliament* in early 1999. This detailed report was credited to a weighty group of some 60 to 70 leading business people, and covered a wide range of ideas and proposals intended to suggest some ways in which Holyrood could help business in Scotland. Brown and McCrone, researching amongst business elites through the period 1998-1999, also report a clear change of attitude. Although they found continuing scepticism, they cite one comment to illustrate a prevailing mood of acceptance among the subjects of their study:

> *Our position prior to the referendum was that the case had not been made from the business point of view. With the referendum having taken place and the settled will of the people expressed, we accepted reality. We must work to see that it works.*

> **(Brown and McCrone, 1999: 142)**

# BUSINESS AND THE COMPETENCIES OF THE SCOTTISH PARLIAMENT

The new Parliament has powers which will impact on business very substantially. There are powers to encourage the development of the Scottish economy and financial resources to support that development, where it is considered appropriate and within its competence. It also has control over education through all ages, and influence over training, both for the employed and the unemployed. Holyrood has legislative competence to promote trade and exports, inward investment and tourism. Some of this will be mediated through the UK Treasury, particularly when Scotland might be tempted into a bidding war for inward investment with Wales, Northern Ireland or one of the new English Regional Development Agencies established earlier in 1999. In effect the legislation is framed in a way which will attempt to maintain a broad parity between the different regions and nations of the UK when it comes to encouraging business location, and the operation of business - the 'level playing field' often argued for by business people.

Because all 'common market' legislative powers are reserved to Westminster the direct and immediate impact of the Parliament on business is actually quite limited. As the former head of the Scottish Office Industry Department, Peter Mackay put it: 'I do believe, on the basis of the current proposals, that the direct impact on business will be very slight' (Leicester, 1997: 7). It is therefore important to consider the extent to which that indirect influence of Holyrood can be far greater than the direct influence on business.

## GOVERNMENT AND BUSINESS

To assess the overall impact of the Parliament, it is important to consider just what any business regime might require or expect from the government and legislature of the jurisdictions within which it operates. The hot blooded simplicities of ' no red tape' are not accepted by the vast majority of business decision makers, who require government to be responsible for developing and maintaining a number of different elements of the business environment. These elements can be the responsibility of different levels of government, either separately or jointly and this division has become even more apparent after the transfer of devolved powers to Holyrood and include:

- a robust and stable currency and banking system;
- consistent and predictable regulation on working conditions, trade descriptions on volume, content and form of products and services;
- a corporate fiscal regime, covering the treatment of profits and losses, incentives and investments and other costs (such as property) which is broadly even handed across the jurisdiction of business domicile;
- a local human and physical infrastructure that is supportive and encouraging of enterprise development in the broadest sense;
- broadly equitable and comparable treatment of residents within the

jurisdiction in relation to the forms of taxation they pay and the benefits they receive through government;
- capacity to intervene to address market weaknesses and failures.

# THE POTENTIAL IMPACT OF THE PARLIAMENT

It may be the case that the most significant implication for business of having to deal with different layers of government will be an increased recognition of the complex inter-relationship between the decisions of those different layers of government and the unintended consequences of their actions. The potential ramifications here are extensive, so just a few illustrations are given (see Table 7) as an example of how the exercise of powers by the Scottish Parliament and other layers of government may have implications for business.

### Table 7: Government Policy and the Business Environment

| Decisions | Levels of Government | Likely outcome for business/action by business |
|---|---|---|
| Decrease rate of corporation tax | Westminster | Reduced tax payments by incorporated businesses |
| Increases in personal tax | Holyrood | Substantial increase in incorporation by sole traders and partnerships. Increase in dividend payments and shift of remuneration to employees from salary to dividend payments on shares |
| Shift of economic development resources within Scottish Enterprise from inward investment incentives to indigenous start- up businesses | Holyrood | Increase in business birth rate with anticipated increase in business innovation, growth and employment prospects |
| Introduction of rates relief (rates 'holiday') for inward investors for five years with a subsequent five year taper reduction in payments | Holyrood and local government | Greater long-term predictability of costs for inward investors with positive impact on inward investment |

| Give powers to local government to introduce new forms of taxation (e.g. tourism bedroom tax), which might be hypothecated for particular purposes | Holyrood and local government | Levied at a flat rate, on standard occupancy assumptions, this will see a small hotel in Edinburgh pay 4-5% of gross revenues in bedroom tax. This will be significantly higher than any foreseeable income tax variation |
|---|---|---|

The point to be stressed is that the Scottish Parliament alone will have little direct impact on business, and the fears stirred up by its powers to vary tax are very far from the only powers that business should be concerned with. CBI Scotland has recently published its views on a *Competitive Scotland* and explicitly recognised the relationship between Holyrood, Westminster and the wider institutions of Europe:

*Much of businesses current concerns are focused on UK/EU policy. But this makes it more, rather than less, important that the Scottish Parliament does not add to these pressures.* (CBI Scotland, 2000)

One of positive aspects of the establishment of a new Parliament is the extent to which procedures and systems will be refreshing different from those of Westminster. The Enterprise and Lifelong Learning Committee certainly broke new ground when it invited business people in Scotland to debate business relations. The chamber on the Mound was full of people from businesses of all sizes and sectors, invited to debate the committee report on support for enterprise and business development. Such an exercise clearly signalled a new way of engaging the business community in public policy, and was welcomed by all those concerned.

## THE FUTURE?

A reasonable judgement on the potential impact of the Scottish Parliament on business in Scotland would be a high degree of anticipation and expectation, but real uncertainty about which levers of influence count and where business should seek to apply such influence.

Previously business has not really needed to be engaged with the institutions of government in Scotland, safe in the knowledge that it could influence decisions through the 'usual channels' at the Scottish Office or in Westminster and Whitehall. This has been changed by the process of devolution and throws down a new challenge to politicians, civil servants and business. Politicians and civil servants have to engage with the wider business community, ranging from the umbrella organisations to major corporate companies and the burgeoning small business sector. In turn, business has to become more involved with government than demanding that government keep out of the way or demanding support for a minimal state, low tax, low regulation agenda. Instead, business must positively ask and engage government in the task of setting out policies and a framework for future economic prosperity and social justice.

Already new relationships are starting to develop, and the future will show us how effective they are. What are also needed are new visions and voices.

# the housing debate

## robina goodlad

The Parliament has still to make an impact on housing policy. A Green Paper was published before the elections and a draft bill is to appear in 2000. In the meantime, the Executive has made the running over the transfer of council housing to alternative landlords and the related proposal for a right to buy for housing association tenants. However, the Parliament has shown itself to be a barometer of Scottish opinion. Debates on the floor and in the Social Inclusion, Housing and Voluntary Sector Committee suggest that the Executive will ignore at its peril the strength of opinion on some housing issues.

New Labour has been determined to tackle under-investment in council housing through transfer of ownership to 'community ownership' landlords, housing associations or other non-profit making bodies with tenants on the board. Additional public investment is tied to transfer, since this method secures more investment for each taxpayer's pound, while offering tenants a new role.

The main mechanism for securing additional investment is New Housing Partnerships (NHPs), which stress tenant involvement, additional resources from the Comprehensive Spending Review, and the commitment to deal with residual debt. The NHP programme includes new building for rent, a transfer of function potentially more significant than stock transfer in the longer term.

Almost one-third of Scotland's 630,000 public sector dwellings - around 200,000 houses - may be transferred to alternative landlords by 2002 or soon after. This initiative would constitute 150,000 NHP transfers, the remaining Scottish Homes stock (14,000) and a trickle of small scale transfers outside the NHP programme. This estimate depends on the success of present intentions to transfer the entire stock of seven authorities, including Glasgow, or an equivalent number of units in smaller scale transfers.

Transfer depends on proposals that can be approved simultaneously by councillors, the Scottish Executive, tenants, financial institutions and new landlords. This approval is hard to achieve and may be made harder if councillors lose confidence that council housing will be protected from the right to buy after transfer. The bill next session will resolve this issue and the conduct of the debate provides a challenge for the Parliament and Executive.

# CHAPTER 19: 'a man's a man for a' that': equality for all in scotland?

**rowena arshad**

The equality agenda of the Scottish Parliament, prior to May 6th 1999 was shaped by two key developments:

- the Scotland Act 1998
- the work of the Consultative Steering Group (CSG)

While the Scotland Act ensured that the UK (Westminster) Parliament retained the right to legislate and make regulations on equal opportunity issues, it also enabled the Scottish Parliament to 'encourage' the observance of these regulations and to impose them as a requirement on public bodies.

More significantly, it included for the first time references to sexual orientation, language, age and social origins, aspects of equality that had previously not been explicitly enshrined in legislative details. As defined in the Scotland Act 1998, equal opportunities means:

> *the prevention, elimination or regulation of discrimination between persons on grounds of sex or marital status, on racial grounds, or on grounds of disability, age, sexual orientation, language or social origin, or of other personal attributes, including beliefs or opinions, such as religious beliefs or political opinion ..*
> **(Scotland Act 1998, Schedule 5, Section L. 2)**

The second significant development were the recommendations of the Consultative Steering Group (CSG) set up by Donald Dewar, Secretary of State for Scotland in November 1997. This cross-party group was charged with the task of considering the operational needs and working methods of Parliament. Its report was published in January 1999 recommending four key principles for Parliament to adopt. The four principles would ensure:

- sharing of power
- accountability
- access and participation
- equal opportunities for all (Consultative Steering Group, 1999: 3)

The CSG invited the Scottish Parliament to endorse these principles which would stand as a symbol of what the Scottish people may reasonably expect from the elected representatives. Parliament duly adopted these principles.

Without a doubt, this fourth principle of the CSG report helped anchor the concept of mainstreaming equality into the work of the Parliament. The Report which was written after a wide ranging consultation exercise across Scotland also recommended that there should be an Equal Opportunities Committee as well as an Equality Unit to provide a focus for these efforts. The remit of the Equal Opportunities Committee would be to develop equal opportunity policies for the Parliament and to scrutinise the delivery and mainstreaming of equal opportunities within the policy making agenda of Parliament. For the first time in the governance machinery of Scotland, equal opportunities was structurally recognised in the shape of a committee and the Unit.

## PRE-MAY 6TH: DARING TO HOPE

Expectations varied. Those in the world of creating policy and particularly equality policy had fairly high expectations for change. For example, the 50/50 campaign run jointly by the Scottish Trades Union Congress (STUC) and the Equal Opportunities Commission (EOC) sought to have a gender balance of male and female MSPs in the first Scottish Parliament. There was an expectation that in the lead up to selection for seats that the various political parties would ensure positive action to achieve gender balance. The 50/50 campaign expected the Scottish Parliament to create an infrastructure that would be more equitable, particularly for those with childcare and caring commitments. There was an expectation that the new Parliament would recognise that parliamentarians had lives outside work and that the pattern of the business day would take cognisance of that. There was also an expectation that the new Parliament would be more diverse and representative of the peoples of contemporary Scotland particularly in relation to ethnicity.

There was an expectation from those who had worked for many years campaigning about justice, human rights and equality that the Scottish

Parliament would deliver on all aspects of equality. Alongside such hope, there were also some fairly low expectations. Such cynicism was borne from years of being excluded, due to a closed and disinterested response from previous Scottish administrations on equality issues.

## A YEAR ON: HAVE THESE HOPES BEEN MET?

In equality terms, there is no doubt that the first year of Parliament will be remembered for its decision to push ahead with the repeal of Clause 2A of the Local Government Act 1986 (more commonly known as Section 28) which tells local authorities not to 'promote' homosexuality (see Evans, 1989-90 on the original background). Clause 2A is seen by many to legitimise intolerance and prejudice particularly on grounds of sexual orientation. The Executive saw the repeal of Clause 2A as removing a piece of legislation that singled out sexual orientation from the statute book.

The speed of the decision to repeal came as a surprise even to the leading gay rights campaigning groups such as the Equality Network. The repeal of Section 28 was certainly one of the key demands from lesbian, gay, bisexual and transgender groups in Scotland but something they did not expect to happen by the second term of Parliament, let alone within the first six months of the first term. The reaction since the government's announcement of its intention to repeal Clause 2A has been alarming. Of particular concern has been the way sections of the community and media have pounced upon the intention to repeal as part of an international conspiracy to kill off family values and foster the 'promotion' of homosexuality. Much misinformation has flowed, resulting in a rise in the number of homophobic attacks and harassment being reported and experienced by gay and lesbian communities in Scotland.

Some might argue that putting controversial issues such as Section 28 on the agenda is foolhardy for a fledgling Parliament but others might applaud the courage of Parliament to open Pandora's box and debate issues which have for a long time been taboo. Yet others might be more cynical and cite this Parliament as merely being 'canny' by moving a step ahead of the European Convention on Human Rights (ECHR), which becomes part of domestic law on October 2nd 2000. Section 28 breaches ECHR and it would have only been a matter of time before repeal was imposed by Europe.

What perhaps has been the most worrying aspect of the Section 28 debate is that Scotland can no longer be smug about its egalitarian credentials. Though

'a man's a man for a' that': equality for all in scotland

the Scottish Executive was right to lead on this human rights issue, it cannot be assumed that the population at large would necessarily buy into the equality agenda nor seek to coherently understand such an agenda.

The debates around Section 28 has masked other equality initiatives as a result of the new Parliament. Some significant developments include:

- Returning 37 per cent women parliamentarians (previously only 11%) - propelling Scotland from near the bottom of the world's gender league table to third from the top.

- Placing equality issues explicitly within a ministerial brief.

- Setting up the Parliament's own Equal Opportunities (EO) Committee within the formal structures of Parliament.

- The Parliament's EO Committee has worked hard since its inception, taking evidence from many community groups and equality bodies such as the Commission for Racial Equality (CRE) and EOC on matters relating to equality. Its most noticeable achievement has been the way in which, through gathering evidence from external groups, it successfully challenged the Scottish Executive for excluding a question on religion. A question on religion is now included in the 2001 Census. The work of the EO Committee has shown that it is possible for parliamentary processes to work effectively and for people to influence decisions.

- Setting up an Equality Unit to support the work of the Executive and promote equal opportunities for all. This Unit launched a national consultation paper *Towards an Equality Strategy* in spring 2000 which is due to formulate strategy by September 2000.

- On December 1st 1999, Donald Dewar committed parliamentarians and the Scottish Parliament to mainstreaming equality within the work of the Parliament by adopting a checklist prepared by the Equal Opportunities Commission (EOC) and the Commission for Racial Equality (CRE) together with the Governance for Scotland Forum, University of Edinburgh. The checklist provides six key questions focussing primarily on the impact of policy on all equality groups.

- Setting up two Ministerial Groups to respond to the Stephen Lawrence Inquiry report - the MacPherson Report. One Group chaired by Jim Wallace, Deputy First Minister, has taken forward action within the Criminal Justice system and Police Authorities. The second group - the Race Equality Advisory Forum (REAF) chaired by Jackie Baillie, Deputy Minister for Communities, will report in autumn 2000 with recommendations on how to take forward race equality work in Scotland including ways of improving consultation with and the participation of black/ethnic minority groups. Both groups have strong black/minority ethnic representation within them.

- The second bill passed into law by the Scottish Parliament, the Adults with Incapacity Bill, includes the first recognition in Scots law of the existence and validity of same-sex partnerships. The bill gives a right to the nearest relative of an adult with incapacity to have a say in their affairs.

- Publication of the document *Social Justice: a Scotland where everyone matters* which clearly commits the Parliament to promoting social justice and equality of opportunity for everyone in Scotland.

There are other initiatives that may not necessarily be seen as equality initiatives, such as the development of Social Inclusion Partnerships, Lifelong Learning, the Homelessness Task Force, local childcare partnerships, family friendly policies and initiatives to counter domestic violence - all of which address issues of inclusion, representativeness and diversity.

## ISSUES AHEAD

It would be too cosy and smug to assume a congratulatory mode to this chapter. Indeed while there have been gains, there have also been major disappointments. For example, the configuration of governance - the make up of the Parliament, civil service and Scottish Executive have remained largely homogeneous. There have been improvements within the gender make-up of governance but not so in relation to race or disability. Despite black/minority ethnic peoples' preparedness to lobby for change and to be representative of change by putting themselves forward for election, the first Scottish Parliament is as it was 300 years ago - all white.

Black/ethnic minority candidates were largely placed in unwinnable seats. Yet political parties who did put up black/ethnic minority candidates unashamedly used them to enhance the party's race equality credentials within communities.

'a man's a man for a' that': equality for all in scotland

This has left many within the black/ethnic minority communities wondering if perhaps it is 'business as usual' and that any change is likely to be cosmetic in terms of racial equality.

Mainstreaming as defined by the EOC and CRE means rethinking provision to accommodate gender, race, disability and other dimensions of equality such as class, sexuality and religion, however it is questionable whether a Parliament and civil service that is homogeneous (particularly in relation to race, disability and class) can effectively mainstream equality issues.

# BRIDGING THE GAP

One of the major gaps to have emerged in the last year has been the lack of concert between many enthusiastic parliamentarians, in power for the first time, fresh and eager to do the best for the Scottish people and the staidness of the Scottish civil service. The McStaidness of the civil service - a combination that comes with a large order of 'gatekeeping' behaviour and an unhealthy portion of resistance to change, has resulted in equality issues not being successfully embedded into all aspects of the Parliament's work.

Mainstreaming equality, despite the clarion call of the First Minister to his parliamentarians to sign up to equality, has largely remained an issue for Ministers with a clear brief for social inclusion and equality, the Parliament's Equal Opportunities Committee and the Executive's Equality Unit. By and large the policy actors within the Executive and the majority of the male parliamentarians are not engaged with the equality debate. The lack of consideration of equality issues within many key reports that have emerged from Parliament within the first year has been stark. The continued invisibility of equality issues across the policy making agenda has to questioned.

Some have used the fact of equal opportunities being a reserved matter to Westminster as an excuse for not addressing equality issues robustly. Others continue to play the numbers game, particularly on an issue such as race where the relatively low numbers of black/ethnic minority people makes race issues a non-vote winner and therefore irrelevant. Others do not engage with equality issues simply because they appear incapable of applying their intellectual prowess and skills to matters of equality in the way they would to other complex issues. Rather than taking every opportunity to build a reserved matter into the framework of Scottish legislation, there appears to be a lack of creativity to seek ways to embed equality into all pieces of work and to seek to influence the UK context in equality matters.

The Standards in Scotland's Schools etc. Bill currently going through Parliament is one such example. Despite numerous submissions by various equality commissions, voluntary sector groups and bodies, there remains a deep reluctance to citing equality explicitly within the bill and to cross-reference the text of the bill to existing equality legislation or to the definition of equal opportunities in the Scotland Act. The concerns of equality practitioners about the lack of inclusion of equal opportunities into this bill have largely been ignored. Questions need to be asked as to why this level of reluctance exists. Those that craft new legislation or policies should be demonstrating how equality issues can be included rather than attempting to block changes.

## CONSULTATION OVERLOAD

There is also worry within the practitioner communities that the Parliament is on consultation overload as regards equality issues. Consultation is necessary but it has the potential danger that consultation becomes a way of absolving those with the responsibility for governance to set out a set of values or a set of responsibilities for society to debate and operate by. A balance will need to be struck between listening to those whose voices have for so long been excluded and unheard, and setting out action plans with measurable targets which will give people evidence that parliamentary processes are robust in affecting change, tackling inequality and discrimination.

Consulting a public that is not informed or is misinformed is unlikely to lead to considered responses. People need to become better informed about a range of issues, including equality related issues. Until that kind of popular political education takes place, an over-reliance on consultative feedback can be dangerous. For example, it is likely, given the lack of racialisation of Scottish politics and the ad hoc manner in which multicultural and anti-racist education is included in the curriculum, that many Scottish people do not see the need to support racial equality (as there is no racism here) nor do they view it a priority (there are so few ethnic minorities here). It is highly likely that the majority just do not understand racial equality issues.

## TOWARDS THE FUTURE

The adoption of the CSG principles, the increased number of women in Parliament, the commitment to family friendly work practices, the formalising of equality through setting up an Equal Opportunities Committee and Unit are indicative of a commitment to equality issues within the Parliament. As it moves

'a man's a man for a' that': equality for all in scotland

towards the end of the first term of office, the following suggestions should be considered to further embed equality onto the Scottish agenda:

- Production of a parliamentary equality action plan with short, mid and long term measurable objectives with clear targets for different departments within the Executive. Such an action plan should take into account various targets for different equality issues. This would assist ownership of equality issues to move beyond those charged with an equality brief within the Parliament or Executive. An annual equality report should be published by Parliament and be available to the Scottish people. This report would monitor whether targets have been met and allow for evaluation of the effectiveness of departmental equality action plans.

- The Equal Opportunities Committee needs to 'win' for itself a more authoritative position and clout, similar to those held by other committees such as the Committee on Enterprise and Lifelong Learning. It needs to stop fire-fighting and begin to be pro-active, and adopt a more strategic overview of the work needing to be done to ensure mainstreaming of equality issues.

- Permanent secretaries of the civil service need to follow the example of the First Minister and issue their own clarion call to civil servants to ensure mainstreaming of all equality issues into the work of the Executive.

- Training in how to mainstream equality issues needs to be provided to parliamentarians as well as civil servants - particularly how mainstreaming equality relates to budget allocations, distribution of structural funds and within the commissioning of research.

- Promote the practice of equality legislation. For example, enact the spirit of the Equal Pay legislation, now 30 years old. Conduct a Pay Audit of the Scottish Executive, its quangos and related service providers and publish findings to ascertain whether the Equal Pay Act is being followed.

- Set up forums for disabled communities and lesbian, gay, bisexual and transgendered peoples, similar to the Women in Scotland Consultative Forum and the Race Equality Advisory Forum. Such forums should also be able to link with the wider Scottish Executive - not just with the Equality Unit or EO Committee.

- Set up a forum which allows the various equality Commissions including the Scottish Human Rights Centre to engage in regular formal dialogue with the Parliament. This would assist collaborative working, reduce duplication and compartmentalisation of issues thereby assisting congruence and partnership.

- Urgently explore how to co-opt experienced people, currently under-represented within the Parliament and Scottish Executive, to assist the work of Parliament and particularly within committee structures.

The mantra of this Parliament is that 'equality is at the heart of government'. A year is a short time to create change and hopes have to be tempered with realism and pragmatism. While equality issues have been taken seriously by some Ministers and members of the Executive, it is by no means uniform. Ultimately however, the litmus test will be whether the people outside the wheel of government feel the impact of a more just and inclusive Scotland.

# ACKNOWLEDGMENTS

My thanks to Philomena de Lima, Malcolm Parnell, Dhamendra Kanani, Morag Alexander, Tim Hopkins, Jackie Baillie and Bob Benson for helping to shape this chapter.

'a man's a man for a' that': equality for all in scotland

# TAG THEATRE COMPANY CONGRESS OF NATIONS: FEEDBACK FROM PUPILS

When the children were asked about what they had learnt from attending the Congress, it was clear that they had learnt much about themselves as well as politics.

*I learnt how not to be scared of speaking up front.*

Pupil from St Gerardine's Primary School, Lossiemouth

*That children can have their own say.*

Anonymous pupil

*I'm confident about talking in front of lots of people.*

Pupil from Ancrum Road Primary School, Dundee

*Before I thought that politics was boring. But now I find it much more interesting.*

Anonymous pupil

*I learnt that they (the MSPs) think that we are the most important people.*

Pupil from Quarrybrae Primary School, Glasgow

*I learnt that everyone has a say, and everyone can present good ideas.*

Anonymous pupil

*That I'm not really shy at all.*

Pupil from Muckhart Primary School, Clackmannanshire

*I was proud that I got to sit on the Presiding Officer's seat and bang the hammer.*

Pupil from Quarrybrae Primary School, Glasgow

*If you ever had a proper visit to the Parliament like us and sat in the MSPs' chairs and voiced your opinion and views of what you would like to change in our country rather than sitting watching it on television I am sure you would feel differently about the Parliament. It widens your knowledge and helps you to understand where immense decisions are made and who develops them. It also helps you to understand the Parliament is more than just boring and you might find you were born to be an MSP. In our time there we have expanded our knowledge of the Parliament a great deal. We all now would like to be MSPs.*

Rachel Smith and Anne-Lise McKenzie, from Davidson's Main Primary School, Edinburgh

# CHAPTER 20: communicating to a new polity: the media and the parliament

### philip schlesinger

It is difficult to overstate the importance that the Scottish media - press, radio and television - have played in keeping the issue of devolution on the agenda, both before the creation of the Parliament and in subsequently shaping public perceptions of the new constitutional settlement since the elections of May 6th 1999 (Meech and Kilborn, 1993; Schlesinger, 1998; Smith, 1994).

What expectations did political press correspondents and broadcasters have before devolution was put in place? A widely-shared view was that the Parliament had to be held accountable. One veteran commentator thought that the press could offer systematic coverage of the new Parliament and penetrate a political process increasingly characterised by 'spin-doctoring' under new Labour. A leading political correspondent observed that 'the political journalists have been living this Parliament for a number of years. We have a stake in it.' One broadsheet editor wanted to move from the obsession with devolution, as he saw it, to a more general political agenda, and to shake up Scottish Labour. Attitudes towards spin doctors were somewhat paradoxical. Scotland was depicted as a backwater in terms of media manipulation by the Scottish Office yet there was widespread confidence that reporters could easily handle effective spinning, were it ever to emerge. Not surprisingly, these views relate more to what would become of the Executive (an assumed continuation of the Scottish Office) than to imagining how media would relate to the Parliament (an institution yet to be born).

Pre-devolution, belief among political journalists in the emergence of a new, consensus politics was hard to detect; nor was fundamental change in how Scotland was governed apparently expected. At best, there were sceptical hopes for a more open and accessible Parliament, roughly in line with the rhetoric of key ministers such as Donald Dewar and Henry McLeish. But if optimism was muted that was because journalists could, and would, point to examples of old-style, divisive politics such as the contentious decision on siting the Parliament at Holyrood rather than Calton Hill. Without a clear image of what the Parliament would bring, after the Scotland Act came into effect, it would be largely, it was reasonable to expect, business as usual in the new Executive. Yet it was also felt that the Parliament did offer something new - a locus for political reporting that could supplant Westminster and would certainly make Scottish politics more interesting.

## THE MEDIA DO A LITTLE LOBBYING

A story to be told in detail elsewhere is how the media lobbied for space on the Mound and how they energetically tried to shape the rules that would govern the reporting of the Parliament (1). It is an important tale because by the Parliament's first session, the in-house broadcasting infrastructure was largely in place and the media's rules of engagement with MSPs broadly set. How did we get to where we are?

Well before the May 1999 elections, the press and broadcasters separately lobbied the Scottish Office. Quite late in the day, these two interests came together under the aegis of the Consultative Steering Group, which set up an Expert Panel on Media Issues that reported in May 1999 (Consultative Steering Group Expert Panel on Media Issues, 1999).

By early 1998, the political press had formed their own lobbying arm, the Scottish Parliamentary Press Association. This group (whose leading lights came from The *Sunday Times*, The *Herald*, and The *Scotsman*) pursued a distinctive agenda in contradistinction to that of the broadcasters. The political press wanted to ensure that commercial lobbyists were prevented from representing themselves as journalists. In some newspaper quarters (but by no means all) there was also a desire to ensure that Scotland did not reproduce the well-known Westminster system of reporting on 'lobby' terms. This wish to be different from London was at the same time coupled with a determination to have privileged access to politicians.

The broadcasters, led by BBC Scotland, were also keen to secure their place in the sun. A group of organisations (including the BBC, BSkyB, Border TV, ITN, Scottish Media Group and Scot FM) reached agreement with the Scottish Office in early 1999 about how to cover the Parliament and the arrangements to be made for the 'feed' - the pictures and sound coming from the debating chamber and committee rooms. The BBC in particular, dissatisfied with the limitations imposed by Westminster rules, pushed hard to ensure that a more flexible style of coverage be developed. This was London's agenda as much as Glasgow's.

# RULES OF COVERAGE

The Expert Panel on Media Issues was essentially a forum for working out the diverse interests of the Scottish press and broadcasting, and steered by Scottish Office civil servants. The broadcasters wanted to show television pictures and conduct interviews from as many locations on the parliamentary campus as they reasonably could. Largely accepted by the Expert Panel, this approach led to the interviews we see in the Black and White Corridor on the Mound and to the relatively fluid style of the camerawork in the debating chamber (at least compared to Westminster). Scotland's style of parliamentary television is quite distinct and maybe this modest achievement has been rather overlooked.

From the start there has been a televisual informality that meshes well with the lack of pomp on the Mound. The political class has embraced the television age, unlike its London counterparts who still regard the camera as an interloper in the Commons. But while much energy was invested in creating a modern broadcast image, how much of it actually comes through the television screen and over the radio? The average viewer will see the odd piece of footage on news bulletins and on low-audience current affairs programmes such as *Holyrood* and *Holyrood Live* on BBC Scotland, *Platform* on Scottish TV, and *Crossfire* on Grampian TV. The radio listener will hear very little directly from Parliament (Garner, 1999). If politicians are seen and heard, it is most often outwith the chamber and most probably in the studio. The usual logics of media coverage mean that watching what goes on in the House - as opposed to how it is reported by political journalists - is going to be a minority pursuit.

For their part, the newspaper political correspondents wanted maximum access to politicians for background information. The Expert Panel decided to recommend to allow access to MSPs by accredited journalists. A Westminster-style 'lobby' system has been formally rejected. But accreditation to the Mound has been restricted only to 'bona fide' reporters. Behind this decision lies correspondents' and editors' belief that some public relations professionals might misrepresent themselves as journalists. They argued that the lines between reporting and advocacy might blur, opening up accusations of 'sleaze' as at Westminster. Journalists covering Parliament have to sign up to a media code of conduct asking them to observe the House's regulations and accepting that they cannot work for lobbyists. This caution has been prescient, as we shall see.

A media relations office was set up in Parliament just before the May 1999 elections. It built on the guidelines developed by the Expert Panel and has become a very busy operation, servicing the daily demands of a media corps of between 30 and 40 political correspondents. The political media do indeed live cheek by jowl with their informants, and have a rather extensive right to roam the corridors of the parliamentary campus from their base in Lawnmarket House. No similar rules of the game were worked out in advance for the media's relations to the Scottish Executive.

## PARLIAMENT UNDER FIRE

Despite the predominance of the medium, it has not been television coverage that has most affected public perceptions of the Parliament, but rather some scathing press coverage. Between the general election on May 6th to the State Opening on July 1st 1999, Parliament had a pasting in the press. Members' reported obsessions with their allowances, seating, demarcation disputes between list and constituency MSPs, and the proposal to take a long summer recess all encountered hostile reporting. The State Opening, with its popular carnival atmosphere, its relative lack of pomp compared to Westminster (although still pretty regal an affair at that), song, poetry and humour, was something of a counterweight to the relentless barrage of criticism. On that occasion the press waxed lyrical. But in general Parliament got off to a bad start and as disputes about the cost of building Holyrood rumble on, it cannot be said that the overall public image is positive.

Concern in the political establishment was signalled in early September 1999, when Sir David Steel, Parliament's Presiding Officer, attacked what he deemed to be misrepresentations of the Mound's approach to controlling costs, members' holidays and their commemorative medallion. He denounced the 'bitch journalism' of the tabloid press, in particular of the *Daily Record*, Scotland's largest selling daily. Complaints referred by Sir David to the Press Complaints Commission were not upheld, and predictably, his strictures led to several papers accusing him of seeking to gag freedom of expression and cover up Parliament's failings. But there was also measured support to be found elsewhere in the media. However, as the *Daily Record* counter-attacked, Sir David found himself rather isolated. He became entangled in a political row about whether he was speaking for himself, or on behalf of Parliament as an institution.

Parliament was also severely tested by media coverage of the so-called 'Lobbygate' scandal, which hit the fledgling institution shortly after the Steel debacle. This was a major public relations crisis that put the credibility and probity of the entire political class on the line.

At the heart of the row was the allegation, made by the *Observer*, that a prominent firm of lobbyists, Beattie Media, could improperly influence Ministers. Beattie employed Kevin Reid, son of the Secretary of State for Scotland, Dr John Reid, as a lobbyist. Public Affairs Europe (a joint venture between Beattie Media and the law firm Mclay Murray Spens) had previously employed Jack McConnell, Minister of Finance in the Scottish Executive, in a public relations and lobbying capacity. Beattie Media employees had supposedly had access to McConnell's official diary through yet another ex-employee working as his constituency secretary. As the political press has a deep suspicion of lobbyists no story could have been more calculated to set them off on a campaign of exposure.

The issue came before Parliament's Standards Committee which decided to hold an inquiry. Not surprisingly, 'Lobbygate' became a major story, with much reporting and commentary on 'sleaze' and the need to avoid Westminster's failings. The *Scotsman* decided to launch a petition to the Court of Session to force the Standards Committee's hearings to be open, although insiders say it was never intended to do more than discuss the terms of reference in private. The Standards Committee exonerated all Ministers named of any wrongdoing. The *Scotsman* withdrew its petition after Parliament published detailed guidelines on procedures for holding committee hearings in private. It is reasonable to doubt that the public followed the nuances, and the big picture was not helpful in building legitimacy.

## 'NO SIX, PLEASE - WE'RE BRITISH!'

If television news has played a supporting role in the dramas of the first year, perhaps that is because it has yet to find its proper place in a devolved polity. For the past two years there has been intermittent debate about the 'Scottish Six' - shorthand for a *Six O'clock News* originated by BBC Scotland to replace the UK-wide networked service from London on BBC1.

The Six's protagonists say it would serve the Scottish public better than the present arrangement, where the *Six O'clock News* overlaps with BBC Scotland's follow-on news and current affairs programme, *Reporting Scotland*. The programme's detractors question the journalistic calibre of BBC Scotland, ask whether the station is adequately resourced and, much more fundamentally, argue that this would rupture the UK-wide news agenda. It is the fear of a separate news encouraging the SNP's independence agenda that lies at the heart of resistance to change. The BBC's governors were split on the question in

1998-99 and the recently departed Director-General, Lord Birt, was said to be very hostile, as were leading Scottish members of the UK Cabinet.

As a compromise, BBC Scotland was denied the Six and given a 20-minute opt-out from *Newsnight* to carry heavy-weight political analysis of the new Parliament and Executive. Launched in autumn 1999, this also has had its detractors, including prominent broadcasters Jeremy Paxman and Kirsty Wark. *Newsnight Scotland*, although limited in scope, has become a short, late-night weekday site for political debate and analysis in Scotland.

With the next UK election in sight, the BBC's peculiar exposure to the political winds has once more become apparent. *Newsnight Scotland* was fiercely attacked by Brian Wilson, Minister of State at the Scotland Office, in February 2000. He reignited a major debate in the Scottish press over the whole question of devolved broadcasting. The casus belli was a story on the role now played by Scottish MPs at Westminster. Wilson's Scotland Office, and especially his boss, John Reid, have been very sensitive about their political standing and widely seen as engaging in turf wars with the Scottish Executive. Wilson broadened his attack to include the proposal for a 'Scottish Six', claiming that BBC Scotland's plans were a step on the road to the break-up of Britain. Previously, this view had always remained either tacit or understated in government circles.

## THE MEDIA, THE PARLIAMENT AND THE UK

Wilson's attack shows how the media politics of devolution are spilling over into the UK as a whole. Another such instance is the furore over the repeal of Section 28/Clause 2A of the Local Government Act, the legislation which bans the 'promotion' of homosexuality in schools. The campaign against repeal kicked off in mid-January 2000, led by Cardinal Winning, head of the Scots Catholic Church, and Brian Souter, millionaire owner of Stagecoach. Their major megaphone was the *Daily Record*, which along with other tabloids, took a prominent role in the Keep the Clause camp. Pooh-poohed at first as Scots backwoods reaction, the campaign also took off in England the following week. The Archbishop of Canterbury and other clerics south of the border banged the drum in favour of 'family values' and the London press and broadcasting took up the story in full cry.

Much the same can be said about the impact of the Cubie report on student fees in higher education. The story has attracted consistent UK-wide attention since the start of 2000. The Scottish Executive's compromise political solution to

Cubie's recommendations was widely covered north and south of the border. The rapidity with which the message was conveyed southwards, and the immediate political reaction, forced the UK Education Secretary, David Blunkett, to come up with his own concessions to poorer students. In this instance, as in the case of Section 28, the mediation of Scottish politics has reshaped the UK's agenda. One unexpected effect of a Scottish Parliament, therefore, has been to play into the new communicative politics of British decentralisation.

We can now think of the political agenda in a devolving UK as becoming increasingly decentred, with some attendant risks of each part of the state becoming more inward-looking. Of course, London will always dominate the scene. We have only to think of the acres of coverage and hours of air-time devoted to Ken Livingstone's ambition to fill the Mayor's shoes to realise that. The story ran big in Scotland and justifiably so, as it is hardly parochial in its implications. This is because the new politics of regionalism embodied in city devolution threaten to set up some tough competition for resources throughout the UK. The image that is portrayed of a nation or region is going to be more and more important in levering political support for claims. Once it becomes a London issue, Scotland's share of the British state's finances - still largely a matter for the anorak tendency - will rapidly be a common talking-point throughout the bars and households of England.

But what of Scotland's public? How well will we be served in the years ahead. It is increasingly clear that the Parliament has been through its baptism of fire, its fledgling phase of institution-building. The policy and legislative agenda is going to become more dense and commanding. Personalities, scandal, sleaze - these will all remain inexhaustible sources of media story-telling. But, I think, on a diminishing scale as we move into the era of real politics. The public's expectations, whatever their reservations, are increasingly centred on Scotland's devolved politics and institutions. To hold public attention - or, if you prefer, to win market share - reporting, commentary and analysis are going to have to rise to the challenge that this shift of intensity implies. And they will, although never uniformly so, for the simple reason that Scotland is more and more obviously a polity in ways that a year ago it was not.

## END NOTE

(1) This study, Political Communication and the Scottish Parliament, was funded by the Economic and Social Research Council in its Devolution Initiative, Award Ref. No. L327253003. I am grateful to David Miller and William Dinan for their helpful comments on this chapter.

# the parliament rap

**fraser doherty and harry perdikou**

Many of the schools participating in Sense of Community continue to work on the project, and more contributions are still developing from the school children. The rap below is from two pupils at Davidson's Main Primary School, Edinburgh.

Ah boom boom ch (carries on throughout the whole rap)

The Scottish Parliament is real cool
We went in there with our school
To learn about our communities
And what we really need to see

About the Education System
And the SCOTTISH PARLIAMENT!!!

The work therein is really hard
They work out things that should be barred
And how the bills then shall be made
And how kids' games should be safely played

They listened so attentively
To all that our group had to say
Involving through co-operation
To help the total population

# CHAPTER 21: reconfiguring the uk and the isles

## robin wilson

Belfast offers an unusual perspective for placing the evolving architecture of these islands under the scan of the telescope. Implicitly, the view is normally from London, treated by default as the centre of the political universe. Introducing Ireland, a fixed 'Anglo-Irish' lens has been applied, which leaves Scotland (Wood, 1994) and Wales outside the field of vision, never mind creating distortions in the view of Northern Ireland.

It was thus not until 1989, remarkably, that a comprehensive history of these islands was published. This work stressed (Kearney, 1989: 4) how Britain and Ireland represented a 'Britannic melting pot' comprising 'a complex of interacting cultures'. But Kearney's pioneering book, recently followed by Davies (1999), was not only an attempt to look at these islands from a range of positions. It was also explicitly directed against nationalist perspectives of all sorts, whether English, Scottish, Welsh or Irish.

The public inability to conceive of these islands in an overall relationship of multi-cultural mutuality remains, however, and it explains an otherwise extraordinary fact. It might have been thought that the dramatic constitutional transformations of recent years - the decentralising reforms internal to the UK plus the integrating north-south structures designated in Ireland would automatically have led to demands for something like a British-Irish Council from a range of quarters. Think, for instance, of the Scottish National Party's interest in the Celtic Tiger phenomenon, or the decision by the Republic of Ireland's government to establish consulates in Edinburgh and Cardiff to engage with the devolved institutions there.

The British-Irish Council was an ideologically inspired proposition from Ulster Unionism to offset the new north-south axis in Ireland and incorporated into the Belfast agreement as such. It was also accepted without question in both capitals that the council would remain stillborn for as long as the other institutions arising from the agreement were suspended. Yet, as regards intra-UK co-ordination, there is only the British-Irish Council and the Joint Ministerial Committee on Devolution - a very thin mechanism for handling inter-governmental relations compared with the multi-faceted arrangements characteristic of Canada and Australia (Cornes, 1999).

# BEYOND NATIONALISM

Intriguingly, however, the failure of the other components of the archipelago outside of Northern Ireland to adequately address these questions of identity and interdependence is in part an explanation for the failure to date to implement the Belfast agreement successfully. Why so?

In so far as the wider constitutional evolution of these islands is discussed, it is normally, as McMillan (1999) points out, in terms of a thesis of inevitable 'break-up', an implied reversion to a 'natural', national, state of affairs. Tom Nairn set this particular ball rolling from a Scottish nationalist perspective (Nairn, 1977) and Davies (1999) tends to endorse it. Within this view, Scotland will (once more) be independent and Ireland (as never before except under British rule) united - though it is worth remarking that the nationalist prism Nairn applied to Northern Ireland in fact led him at the time to anticipate the consolidation of partition, on the premise that Ireland's completing nationalist claims were utterly incompatible.

As for Northern Ireland, it goes without saying that any theory which suggests a reversion to four basic national identities - English, Scottish, Irish, Welsh - is unlikely to contribute constructively to a peace process which demands respectful recognition of both the Catholic-Irish and British-Unionist identities in the province; indeed, it comes perilously close to the traditional, patronising and (for Unionists) insulting nationalist view that the British identity of Ulster Unionists is a kind of delusion, from which they will recover on the day they bring themselves to admit that they have really been Irishmen all along.

This problem is compounded by a clear privileging of certain nationalisms in the contemporary cultural mosaic (McMillan, 1999: 289):

*At the moment, Scottish and Irish nationalism are routinely seen as fashionable, positive and authentic, whereas 'being British' - in the*

*years after 1945 a general byword for all that was brave and admirable*
*- is currently dead in the water as a moral value and as a style item.*

Yet, apart from any other considerations, for ethnic minorities in the UK, there is simply nowhere else to go.

The solution lies beyond the nationalist paradigm. Nationalists are guilty of a number of delusions which block out more constructive approaches to difference than never-ending wars of attrition - hot or cold. First, an essentially homogeneous category called 'the people' is constituted, identified as having a corporate existence over and above the individual members of a society. Secondly, each such people is designated as having a 'national mission' even if, at times 'the people' have to be 'awakened' to realise it - such as the securing, or sustaining, of its sovereignty. Thirdly, sovereignty is perceived in a zero-sum fashion: either a people has it or somebody else (illegitimately) does. Within such linked assumptions, of course, it is very simple for a very small group, not part of 'the people' - asylum-seekers, say, who pitch up at Dover to become the focus of a moral panic because of the 'threat' they are perceived to represent to (in this case English) national homogeneity, mission and sovereignty.

Yet these are all ideological moves. 'The people' does not exist outside of totalitarian regimes: only diverse and complex citizens inhabit a democracy. It cannot be assumed that they should be recruited, willy-nilly, to a national mission they may or may not endorse. Nor, in a simultaneously devolving and integrating world, can the sovereignty of the 'nation-state' any longer be defined in absolute terms.

## 'THE BRITISH QUESTION'

Linda Colley gave an end-of-millennium lecture in Downing Street on 'Britishness in the 21st century' (Colley, 1999). Homogenising 'cool Britannia' metropolitan hyperbole was inappropriate, she argued, to 'a multi-national, multi-cultural, infinitely diverse polity'. She told the Prime Minister:

*I am not advocating giving up on Britain as a political unit, nor ceasing to re-think it. I propose to you a crucial distinction which is often insufficiently understood: that between identity and citizenship. Instead of being so mesmerised by debates over British identity, it would be far more productive to concentrate on renovating British*

*citizenship, and on convincing all these inhabitants of these islands*
*that they are equal and valued citizens irrespective of whatever*
*identity they may individually select to prioritise.*

A key element in this project for Colley, as for others (Tomaney and Mitchell, 1999), is to avoid the 'nightmare scenarios of a new, embittered English nationalism, or a fully-fledged English Parliament' by pursuing a democratic regionalism, 'far beyond the purview' of the current regional development agencies.

From an Irish perspective, Colley's argument allows the understated reference in the agreement to citizens in Northern Ireland being 'accepted as Irish or British, or both, as they may so choose' to be given its real significance. In fact, within a nationalist perspective, it is impossible to be both: it can only be either/or. And nor can one choose, any more than one can choose one's blood type.

Unionism in Northern Ireland has traditionally tended towards a 'conservative nationalism' (Miller, 1995: 124) of a Powellite kind (Powell became, of course, a popular Ulster Unionist MP after he became persona non grata in the Conservative Party):

*At the core of conservative nationalism stands the idea that national*
*identity integrally involves allegiance to authority. To think of*
*oneself as British [in this view] is ipso facto to acknowledge the*
*authority of institutions such as the monarchy which form the*
*substance of national life.*

There is no point in asking Northern Ireland unionists to stop being unionist: such a mass, quasi-religious conversion is implausible. But they can be asked to redefine their unionism in such a way that they see themselves as British citizens rather than subjects, which would both allow them space to embrace an identity as Irish and discourage them from seeking to subject their fellow citizens to such indignities as loyal-order marches through predominantly Catholic areas.

As for nationalists in Northern Ireland, again it is pointless to hope they may one day acquire an allegiance to the British state: their Irish identity is historically embedded and deeply felt. But they can be asked to redefine their sense of Irishness in such a fashion as would permit all those resident on the island, in whichever jurisdiction, to share an attachment to Irishness in a pluralist manner,

reconfigurating the uk and the isles

rather than it having a cramping, northern, communal flavour (which many southern Irish citizens, never mind northern Protestants, find 'foreign').

## HOMAGE TO CATALONIA

It is through this distinction between identity and citizenship, ethnos and demos, that a resolution of the Northern Ireland problem can be found. Catalonia provides a benign contrast. Whereas opinion surveys in Northern Ireland find responses to questions of identity and allegiance to be highly polarised, Moreno's research on Catalonia (Moreno et al, 1998) identified a continuous spectrum in which the largest group of respondents were those categorising themselves as 'as much Catalan as Spanish'. This does not, of course, eliminate tensions between Barcelona and Madrid, but it does allow these to be constructively played out in contrast to the sterile relationship between the capital and the Basque country, where ETA has largely copied the IRA's 'peace strategy' associated with intensified nationalist protagonism.

Like Spain after Franco, the UK has more recently been undergoing a process of asymmetric devolution (Elcock and Keating, 1998). This is not uncommon: the different regional/national components of heterogeneous states will by definition have differential histories - the position of Quebec in the Canadian federation being an obvious example. What is idiosyncratic is the (very English) 'muddling through' which has characterised the UK process unlike, for example, the Autonomous Communities Act in Spain which set out a permissive framework under which regions/nations could variously draw down powers.

Such autonomy allows either/or conceptions of sovereignty to be superseded. Hence the continuing success of the Catalan nationalist leader, Jordi Pujol. As Guibernau (1997: 109) has argued:

*The relevance of Pujol's nationalism stems from the assumption that it is possible for a nation to live and develop within a multinational state if this state is genuinely democratic and allows enough space for its nations to feel represented and cultivate their difference. This is an innovative conception which could contribute to the resolution of nationalism in some areas, particularly since it seems politically unviable to suddenly multiple the number of states covering the world.*

Part of the difficulty in the UK is the hegemony of English Euro-scepticism, associated with a conception of the British state as unitary rather than a union, whose emblematic institutions - the monarchy, the City, Parliament, warm beer - can only be perceived as threatened by a Euro-invasion. The constrained introduction of English regionalism has betrayed this lack of understanding of the nature of 'multi-level governance' (regional/state/supranational) in the European Union. And hence the unnecessarily fraught character of the debate over Scotland.

On the eve of the elections to Holyrood, Lindsay Paterson suggested at a seminar in Edinburgh that the will-Scotland-become-independent question that had marked the devolution process (on both sides) might turn out, in the long run, to be the wrong question. It would only in reality become relevant when a non-Conservative majority in Edinburgh once more faced a Conservative majority in London - a prospect some years off. Meantime, the key powers reserved to Westminster under the Scotland Act - macro-economic policy, defence and foreign affairs - might well have been transferred to the EU level, via economic and monetary union and the outworking of the war in Kosovo. In which case, Westminster and Whitehall would represent just another set of institutions with which the Edinburgh Parliament had to deal. What, then, would 'independence' versus 'the union' actually mean?

An analogous argument can be made about Northern Ireland. With the republic already prospering inside the euro zone and having accepted that neutrality does not preclude membership of Partnership for Peace, 'sovereignty' is now seen by its increasingly confident citizens as something to be shared rather than sought - including with Northern Ireland (now a depressed basket-case by comparison). Meanwhile, the proliferating 'Maze Europe' regime of cross-border/inter-regional/trans-national arrangements across the EU (Christiansen, 1999) provides a highly favourable environment for the pursuit of all-Ireland policy co-ordination. The sovereignty differential, between devolution and north-south bodies on the one hand, and a united Ireland in Europe on the other, may thus become a fine one by the time northern nationalists had their opportunity to vote in a referendum for the latter. That opportunity - conditional as it is upon there being a likely majority for change in the view of the Northern Ireland Secretary - could be even further off than in Scotland.

# VARIABLE GEOMETRY

Asymmetric devolution, the European context and the evolution of both, mean that the concept of 'variable geometry' normally applied to European integration can best describe the interrelationships within these islands and their change over time. As regards Northern Ireland it removes the zero-sum constitutional premise for the enduring conflict while allowing for organic, consensual change. It enables Northern Ireland to be a region in its own right, part of the Irish 'nation' as well as part of the British state and part of Europe.

But such a benign outcome is only possible if across these islands the temptation to replace centuries of British state centralism by a nationalist regression is avoided. The corollary is an embrace of hybrid identity, a balancing of autonomy and reciprocity, and an acceptance of multi-level governance. So necessary in Northern Ireland, these requirements may apply with just as much force to the rest of the UK and Ireland.

The case for devolution to regions (or small nations) is one that is very well made. Apart from the democratic argument, much economic literature in recent years (for example, Danson, 1997; Cooke and Morgan, 1998) has stressed how the regional level can offer the best opportunity to build the networks of trust-based relationships on which successful development depends. But it would be wrong to fail to recognise that there is an inherent tension in devolution: there are economies of democratic scale which cannot be ignored. Thus, if one imagines the references to 'Scotland' and 'Scottish' being replaced by 'Northern Ireland', the comments of Hassan (1998: 11) perfectly apply there too:

*Scotland is a small country with limited resources and skills in most areas from intellectual activity to politics, culture and sport. The forces of Scottish civil society, whether they be think-tanks, the voluntary sector or other institutions, do not have the financial or infrastructure supports to develop major research departments or projects, and nor do the political parties.*

Policy networks must therefore straddle 'national' boundaries if the potential benefits of sharing of good practice, of dissemination of innovation, of co-ordination and co-operation are to be captured. But this cannot be left to chance. Worse, the danger that reversion into national identity would mean a regression into nationalism, and there would be many issues, such as revision of the Barnett Formula for allocation of public finance, which could easily spark it, is a risk that should be avoided. If the British-Irish Council did not exist as a result of the Belfast agreement, therefore, it would have to be invented (Hassan and

Wilson, 1999). Whatever the fate of the most volatile region in these islands, the council must have an existence independent of the fate of the Good Friday Agreement even in these optimistic post-devolution times. Belfast is not, any more than London, the centre of the universe.

# the land question

## andy wightman

Arguably the most distinctive area of the Parliament's first tranche of legislation is land reform. A topic for so long marginalised and neglected, is now mainstream and we have the Parliament and the Executive to thank for making it so. But there is growing cause for alarm at the caution and timidity emerging from Holyrood. Feudal abolition and national parks are low key and have been long in the gestation and it is the community right-to-buy which is the first major foray into reforming the landed power structures which lie at the heart of the land question. Here evidence grows of a lack of radicalism and purpose and a growing sense that such powers as will be created will make little, if any, change to the way Scotland is owned.

Perhaps the clearest sign yet of the Executive's lack of coherent political philosophy on the land question was its response to the proposed sale of the Cuillin on Skye by John MacLeod of MacLeod. The Executive, faced with the opportunity to construct a coherent political philosophy, paused, retreated and ran for the safe cover of civil service briefings.

As the *Sunday Herald* put it so well in a leader on April 9th 2000:

> *John MacLeod has delivered a political opportunity on a plate but our Ministers do not look eager to dine ... Expert legal opinion, district valuer's prices and compulsory purchase are all in the Executive's armoury before a single sentence of land legislation reaches the statute books. It is time for Ministers to slip the leash, to show their teeth to the lairds and their radicalism to Scotland.*

We still await such a move and beyond that, the more radical agenda of, for example, giving children the right to inherit land, banning offshore trusts, ending absentee landlordism, and regulating the land market.

# CHAPTER 22: the unfinished business of devolution

## robert hazell

The unfinished business of devolution lies at the centre, and can be located in the English Question. England remains the hole in the devolution settlement:

> *The English have been the silent and uninvited guests at the devolutionary feast. Scotland has a Parliament, Wales an Assembly, while England only gets some regional quangos. When Rover collapsed, who was there to speak (and act) for the West Midlands? A striking feature of the devolution legislation has been its total neglect of the union (and English) dimension.* *(Wright, 2000: 11)*

This final chapter is about the Union and the English dimension. It will focus on constitutional architecture, because devolution has left us with some lop-sided political structures. Rebalancing is required, particularly at the centre, if devolution is to be built on firm foundations. Some of this work is now in hand, but in a haphazard way: filling in the rest of the devolution design is being done by a process of patchwork, with no strong sense of constitutional design.

## THE ENGLISH QUESTION

In constitutional terms the English Question is best approached as a series of questions about English representation in our new quasi-federal system:

- should there be an English Parliament to match the Scottish Parliament and the Welsh and Northern Ireland Assemblies?
- should England instead be divided into eight or so regions, each with its own assembly, which in population terms would come much closer to the size of the devolved assemblies?

- or should Westminster be adapted to give greater voice to English concerns, without going as far as creating a separate English Parliament?

# AN ENGLISH PARLIAMENT?

An English Parliament is not a realistic option. Those who demand one are in effect demanding a full-blown federation, in which the four historic nations would form the component parts. But there is no successful federation in the world where one of the parts is greater than one-third of the whole. England with four-fifths of the population would be hugely dominant: even more dominant than Prussia in the old Germany. It would be grotesquely over-balanced, with the English Parliament as important as the Westminster Parliament. Nor is there any strong public demand: William Hague has attracted no more support for the idea (Hague, 1998) than have the Campaign for an English Parliament, during their Wednesday vigils waving their St George's flags in Parliament Square.

The Campaign is a political gesture, making a political point as much as it is pressing for the establishment of a new political institution. The point is that with devolution the Scots, the Welsh and the Northern Irish will have a louder political voice, and the English risk losing out. But the answer for the English lies in adapting Westminster and Whitehall, in ways discussed below, and not in a separate English Parliament.

# REGIONAL ASSEMBLIES FOR ENGLAND

Regional assemblies are one of Labour's two unfulfilled promises from their 1997 manifesto. The manifesto commitment was as follows:

> *Demand for directly elected regional government so varies across England that it would be wrong to impose a uniform system. In time we will introduce legislation to allow the people, region by region, to decide in a referendum whether they want directly elected regional government. Only where clear popular consent is established will arrangements be made for elected regional assemblies ...* **(Labour Party, 1997: 34-35)**

In government it fell to John Prescott to implement this pledge, but he has had little support from his colleagues, and none from No. 10. In the first year the government decided to legislate for Regional Development Agencies but not to create statutory Regional Chambers, which might have proved the first step towards regional government. The government is probably right in its judgement about the lack of public demand, although things are beginning to stir in the regional undergrowth.

Spring 2000 saw the launch of the Campaign for the English Regions, formed by the vanguard regional bodies of the North East, North West, the West Midlands and Yorkshire. The North East is making the running, and in direct imitation of Scotland, three of the regions have established Constitutional Conventions. So far none has got beyond sloganising: there is nothing like the detailed planning about powers, functions and composition which went into the work of the Scottish Constitutional Convention. A referendum in this Parliament is no longer possible; and even in the next the North of England Assembly will face some high hurdles. Under the evolutionary policy proposed by Labour before the election, a Regional Chamber would have to satisfy four conditions before it could become a directly elected Regional Assembly:

- a predominantly unitary structure in local government;
- approval by Parliament;
- approval in a region-wide referendum;
- auditors confirmation that no additional public expenditure overall is involved.

Since the election a further challenge has emerged in the form of directly elected Mayors. Despite the Livingstone setback, these are still strongly championed by No. 10. They are not necessarily incompatible, but there is an interesting tension between the two models. For at regional level there may not be room for two political leaders claiming to be the voice of the region; one as leader of the Regional Assembly and the other as the Mayor of the largest city. Which model wins through may depend upon who occupies the political space first.

At present the elected Mayors look likely to get there first. The enabling legislation should be in place from autumn 2000, the government wants to see more, and other cities could opt for elected Mayors from 2001 onwards. Regional Assemblies are a long way further back, and must first pass through the antechamber of indirectly elected Regional Chambers. Elected Mayors, as the leaders of the biggest local authority in the region, may prove to be one more voice that discovers little interest in moving to a Regional Assembly once they realise that it would be a countervailing source of power over which they would have less control.

the unfinished business of devolution

# THE HOLE IN THE CENTRE: (1) THE IMPACT OF DEVOLUTION ON WESTMINSTER

Post-devolution Westminster is gradually coming to terms with its new role as a quasi-federal Parliament, but in a series of unconnected initiatives and experiments, with no effective lead being offered by the government.

In the House of Commons it was left to the Procedure Committee to conduct an inquiry into the Procedural Consequences of Devolution. The government's initial memorandum and subsequent response to the committee was minimalist, and the committee's report (House of Commons Procedure Committee, 1999) skirted round most of the bigger questions. While wishing to undertake a full review in due course, the committee's initial recommendations included:

- abolition of the Scottish, Welsh and Northern Irish Grand Committees;
- new rules restricting questions to the Scottish and Welsh Secretaries to matters relating to their reduced responsibilities;
- a new procedure for bills relating exclusively to one part of the kingdom, with a special Second Reading Committee.

Absent from the committee's report was any attempt to re-think the role of Scottish, Welsh and Northern Irish MPs post-devolution, to contemplate a reduction in their numbers if their role was found to have diminished, or to address the West Lothian Question. Scottish MPs in particular feel a lost tribe at Westminster. Their numbers are to be reduced in the next Boundary Commission review, from 72 to 60 or less; but no one has addressed the need to make a similar reduction in the number of Welsh MPs, even though Wales is equally over-represented (with 40 MPs, when an equal quota would supply 33). And although the government, in the person of Lord Irvine, says that the only answer to the West Lothian Question is to stop asking it, an answer cannot be postponed for ever - because one day there will be a government at Westminster which depends for its majority on Scottish and/or Welsh MPs. There could then be a political impasse if Scottish MPs continue to determine policy on English health and education, when English MPs can no longer vote on such issues in Scotland.

Part of the solution may lie in Westminster gradually developing its role as a proxy for an English Parliament within the wider shell of the Union Parliament. Pre-devolution it was clear when Westminster was operating in Scottish mode;

post-devolution it may need to become clearer when Westminster is operating in English mode. Over the next few years we will witness greater recognition and formalisation of English business at Westminster, through the work of the Select Committees many of which are de facto English Committees; the recent proposal to revive the Standing Committee on Regional Affairs (which once again could provide a forum for English regional debates, as it did in the 1970s); and through the new experiment of a Main Committee sitting in the Grand Committee Room off Westminster Hall, (House of Commons Modernisation Committee, 1999) which may also provide a forum for English debates.

These initiatives are part of the process of piecemeal adaptation. One issue to watch is who attends these debates. Will Scottish and Welsh Members stay away from English debates and matters which are of no interest to them? And will any such MPs follow the self-denying ordinance set by Tam Dalyell and decline to vote on such issues? If all the Scottish, Welsh and Northern Ireland MPs were to follow Tam's example, William Hague's slogan of English votes on English laws would have been achieved, but by a new convention rather than making the change by law.

Just as important are the potential new roles for the House of Lords. In a quasi-federal Britain one obvious role would be to represent the nations and regions, as second chambers in federal systems represent the states and the provinces. The Wakeham Commission on Lords Reform came down against a full-blown federal solution, but recommended that a minority of the members of a reformed second chamber (ranging from 12 to 35 per cent) should be elected to represent the nations and regions (Royal Commission on the Reform of the House of Lords, 2000). The proportion of elected members is too small, but the principle is right that the second chamber could play an important role in helping to bind together the newly devolved nations and regions with the centre. To strengthen this role Wakeham also recommended that the upper house should have a Devolution Committee, and a Constitutional Committee; and more generally should act as a guardian of the constitution and of the devolution settlement.

# THE HOLE IN THE CENTRE: (2) PRESSURE ON THE COURTS

Devolution brings new pressures to all three branches of central government. The courts will play a central part in interpreting and shaping the devolution settlement, and will themselves come under much greater public scrutiny. They will experience a significant increase in workload and will be called upon to adjudicate in high profile devolution disputes. Will the courts be able to take the strain?

The pressures have already been evident in Scotland, with the surge of human rights cases under the Scotland Act 1998. At the centre the strain will be particularly great in the higher courts, the Judicial Committee of the Privy Council and the Appellate Committee in the House of Lords, where the law lords have recently announced their intention to recruit 'American style' research assistants to help ease the load. But devolution will also impose pressures of a different kind. It will require a strong legal system, and a system which commands respect on all sides, to hold the Union together when the politics comes under strain. In this respect the choice of the Judicial Committee of the Privy Council as the final arbiter of devolution disputes looks decidedly odd. It is not the final court of appeal in the UK legal system, but stands largely outside it; and its constitutional jurisdiction in the rest of the Commonwealth has declined almost to zero. It may prove to be a temporary arrangement which will be re-opened when wider reform of the House of Lords opens up the question of whether we now need a supreme court which stands clearly at the apex of the legal system and outside the legislature.

## THE HOLE IN THE CENTRE: (3) FURTHER ADJUSTMENTS IN WHITEHALL

The third branch of central government which needs to adjust to devolution is the executive branch in Whitehall. Here too the adjustments have been minimalist and piecemeal. There continue to be three territorial Secretaries of State, although post-devolution there is much less justification for separate representation of Scotland, Wales and Northern Ireland in the British Cabinet. The office of Scottish Secretary is the most redundant, given the nature of the devolution settlement in Scotland, but in which order the posts wither away will depend more on the politics of Cabinet formation than on the logic of devolution. But the logic says these posts are redundant: if in ten years' time we still have territorial Secretaries of State then devolution will have failed.

The rump offices of the three territorial Secretaries of State may initially be merged, but in time they will fall back into the Cabinet Office. The Constitution Secretariat will in time become the equivalent of the Department of Inter-governmental Affairs in the Canadian Privy Council Office, which manages federal-provincial relations. It will work to a single Minister, combining the roles of the territorial Secretaries of State, who will be responsible for relations with all the devolved government.

This machinery is gradually falling into place. The main elements were published in the Memorandum of Understanding and first four Concordats between the UK, Scottish and Welsh administrations in October 1999 (Memorandum of Understanding, 1999). The keystone is the Joint Ministerial Committee (JMC) on devolution, which brings together representatives of the UK and devolved government. The JMC will meet in plenary form once a year, chaired by the Prime Minister; and in 'functional' format as meetings of Agriculture Ministers, Environment Ministers etc. as necessary.

## HOLDING THE UNION TOGETHER

The focus in this final chapter has been on institutions and constitutional architecture. Equally important in terms of unfinished business is the need to explain the devolution settlement to the public in all parts of the kingdom. These are fundamental changes in our system of government which have been introduced with a minimum of explanation. For electoral reasons Labour has kept remarkably silent about its plans for constitutional reform. The English could be forgiven for thinking that devolution is some special deal for the Scots, the Welsh and the Northern Irish because no one has troubled to tell them otherwise. Their goodwill should not be taken for granted for ever.

# REFERENCES

Baur, C . (1996) '£17bn says 'Yes'', Insider, October.

Black, R. (2000) Supporting Democratic Scrutiny by Public Audit, London: Public Management and Policy Association.

Blunkett, D. (2000) 'Influence or Irrelevance: can social science improve Government?', Secretary of State's ESRC Lecture Speech, February 2nd.

Brogan, B. (1999) 'The irony of Rafferty', The Herald, December 16th.

Brown, A. Curtice, J. Hinds, K. McCrone, D. Park, A. Paterson, L. and Surridge, P. (forthcoming 2001) New Scotland, New Politics, Edinburgh: Edinburgh University Press.

Brown, A. and McCrone, D. (1999) Business and the Scottish Parliament Project, Edinburgh: Governance of Scotland Forum, University of Edinburgh.

Brown, A. McCrone, D. Paterson, L. and Surridge, P. (1999) The Scottish Electorate: The 1999 General Election and Beyond, Basingstoke: Macmillan.

Brown, T. (2000) 'Father of the Nation', New Statesman Scotland, February 14th.

Burrows, N. (1999) 'The Scottish Executive' in G. Hassan (ed) A Guide to the Scottish Parliament: The Shape of Things to Come, Edinburgh: Centre for Scottish Public Policy/The Stationery Office, 57-63.

Buxton, J. (1996) 'The price of nationalism', Financial Times, April 22nd.

Chisholm, M. (2000) Newsletter to North Edinburgh and Leith constituency, March.

Christiansen, T. (1999) 'The bigger picture', in R. Wilson (ed) No Frontiers: North-South Integration in Ireland, Belfast: Democratic Dialogue, 28-53.

Colley, L. (1999) 'Millennium Lecture: Britishness in the 21st century', Downing Street.

Commission on Local Government and the Scottish Parliament (1999) Moving Forward: Local Government and the Scottish Parliament, Edinburgh: The Stationery Office.

Confederation of British Industry (CBI) Scotland (2000) Competitive Scotland, Glasgow: CBI Scotland.

Consultative Steering Group (1999) Shaping Scotland's Parliament: Report of the Consultative Steering Group, Edinburgh: The Stationery Office.

Consultative Steering Group Expert Panel on Media Issues (1999) Supplementary Report, Edinburgh: The Scottish Office, n.d., but circulated on May 12th 1999.

Consultative Steering Group Working Party (1999) Code of Conduct Report, Edinburgh: The Stationery Office.

Cooke, P. and Morgan, K. (1998) The Associational Economy: Firms, Regions and Innovation, Oxford: Oxford University Press.

Cornes, R. (1999) 'Intergovernmental relations', in R. Hazell (ed) Constitutional

Futures: A History of the Next Ten Years, Oxford: Oxford University Press, 156-177.

Curtice, J. and Park, A. (2000) ' Will devolution make a difference? Scotland's first election and the theory of first order elections', paper presented at the Annual Conference of the Political Studies Association of the UK, London School of Economics.

Curtice, J., Seyd, B., Park A., and Thomson, K. (2000) Wise after the Event? Attitudes to Voting Reform following the 1999 Scottish and Welsh Elections, Constitution Unit Briefing, University College, London.

Curtice, J. and Steed, M. (forthcoming 2000) 'And now for the Commons? Lessons from Britain's first experience with Proportional Representation', in P. Cowley, D. Denver, A. Russell and L. Harrison (eds) British Elections and Parties Review 10, London: Frank Cass.

Danson, M. (ed) (1997) Regional Governance and Economic Development, London: Pion.

Davies, N. (1999) The Isles: A History, London: Macmillan.

Denver, D. Mitchell, J. Pattie, C. Bochel, H. (2000) Scotland Decides: The Devolution Issue and the Scottish Referendum, London: Frank Cass.

Dinwoodie, R. (1999) 'The Empire Strikes Back', The Herald, July 26th.

The Economist (1999) 'Undoing Britain', The Economist Special Issue, November 6th.

Elcock, H. and Keating, M. (eds) (1998) Remaking the Union: Devolution and British Politics in the 1990s, special issue of Regional and Federal Studies, vol 8, no 1.

Enterprise and Lifelong Learning Committee (1999) Inquiry into the Delivery of Local Economic Development Services in Scotland: Interim Conclusions Phase 1, Edinburgh: The Stationery Office.

European Committee (2000) Forward Work Programme for January 2000 to June 2001, special report not published, web edition.

European Committee (2000) 4th Report, 2000 Report on Mainstreaming Environmental Issues Into Government Policy in Scotland: A Contribution to the Debate on the European Commission's 6th Environmental Programme - Initial Findings, SP Paper 108, Session 1(2000), Edinburgh: The Stationery Office.

Evans, D. T. (1989/90) 'Section 28: Law, Myth and Paradox', in Critical Social Policy: A Journal of Socialist Theory and Practice in Social Welfare, Issue 27 Vol. 9 No. 3, 73-95.

Executive Secretariat (1999) The Scottish Executive: A Guide to Collective Decision Making, Edinburgh: Executive Secretariat.

Garner, K. (1999) 'Muted Proceedings: Scottish Radio Broadcasting's Response to the New Scottish Parliament', paper presented at 'Radiocracy: Radio,

Democracy and Development', at the School of Journalism, Media and Cultural Studies, Cardiff University, November 26th-28th1999.

Giddens, A. (1998) The Third Way: The Renewal of Social Democracy, Oxford: Polity.

Guibernau, M. (1997), 'Images of Catalonia', Nations and Nationalism, vol 3, no 1, 89-111.

Hague, W. (1998) Speech to Centre for Policy Studies, London, February 24th 1998.

Hardie, A. (1999) 'Dewar's Speech Adds Fuel to Row Over Role of Committees', The Scotsman, November 10th.

Hardie, A. (2000) 'Anger at plan to axe committees', The Scotsman, May 11th.

Hassan, G. (1998) The New Scotland, London: Fabian Society.

Hassan, G. and Warhurst, C. (1999) 'Tomorrow's Scotland' in G. Hassan and C. Warhurst (eds) A Different Future: A Modernisers' Guide to Scotland, Edinburgh: Centre for Scottish Public Policy/The Big Issue in Scotland, 1-11.

Hassan, G. and Wilson, R. (1999) The British-Irish Council as a Multi-Form Organisation, Edinburgh: Centre for Scottish Public Policy.

House of Commons Modernisation Committee (1999)Sittings of the House in Westminster Hall, HC 194, London: The Stationery Office.

House of Commons Procedure Committee (1999) Procedural Consequences of Devolution, HC 185, London: The Stationery Office.

House of Commons Scottish Affairs Select Committee (1998) The Operation of Multi-Layer Democracy, HC 460-1, London: The Stationery Office.

HM Treasury (1999) Funding the Scottish Parliament, National Assembly for Wales and Northern Ireland Assembly, London: The Stationery Office.

Independent Committee of Inquiry into Student Funding (1999) Student Finance: Fairness for the Future, Edinburgh: The Stationery Office.

John Wheatley Centre (1997) Quangos: Policy Options for a Scottish Parliament, Edinburgh: John Wheatley Centre.

Kearney, H. (1989) The British Isles: A History of Four Nations, Cambridge: Cambridge University Press.

Labour Party (1997) New Labour: Because Britain Deserves Better, London: The Labour Party.

Leicester, G. (1997) Scotland's Parliament: A Business Guide to Devolution, Edinburgh: Scottish Council Foundation.

Leicester, G. and McKay, P. (1998) Holistic Government: Options for a Devolved Scotland, Edinburgh: Scottish Council Foundation.

Lynch, P. (forthcoming 2000) Scottish Government and Politics: An Introduction, Edinburgh: Edinburgh University Press.

McCrone, G. (1999) 'Scotland's Public Finances', in G. Hassan and C. Warhurst (ed), A Different Future: A Modernisers' Guide to Scotland, Edinburgh: Centre for Scottish Public Policy/The Big Issue in Scotland, 116-124.

McMillan, J (1999), 'Britishness after devolution', in G. Hassan and C. Warhurst (eds) A Different Future: A Modernisers' Guide to Scotland, Edinburgh: Centre for Scottish Public Policy/The Big Issue in Scotland, 285-294.

MacMillan, J. (2000), Scotland's Shame, in T. M. Devine (ed) Scotland's Shame?: Bigotry and Sectarianism in Modern Scotland, Edinburgh: Mainstream, 13-24.

Macwhirter, I. (2000a) 'Beware the rise of the Lumpen Scot', Sunday Herald, April 23rd.

Macwhirter, I. (2000b) 'The long journey back from a dangerous humiliation', Sunday Herald, May 7th.

Meech, P. and Kilborn, R. (1993) 'Media and Identity in a Stateless Nation: the Case of Scotland', Media, Culture and Society, vol. 14, no. 2, 245-259.

Memorandum of Understanding (1999) Memorandum of Understanding and Supplementary Agreements between the UK Government, Scottish Ministers and the Cabinet of the National Assembly for Wales, Cm 4444, London: The Stationery Office.

Midwinter, A. (1999) 'The Barnett Formula and Public Spending in Scotland: Policy and Practice', Scottish Affairs, no. 28, Summer 1999, 83-92.

Miller, D. (1995) On Nationality, Oxford: Clarendon.

Mooney, G. and Johnstone, C. (2000) 'Poverty, Inequality and the Scottish Parliament', Critical Social Policy: A Journal of Theory and Practice in Social Welfare, Issue 53 Volume 20 (2), 155-182.

Moreno, L. Arriba, A. and Serrano, A. (1998) 'Multiple identities in decentralised Spain: the case of Catalonia', Regional and Federal Studies, vol 8, no 3, 65-88.

Nairn, T. (1977) The Break-up of Britain: Crisis and Neo-nationalism, London: New Left Books.

Nairn, T. (2000) After Britain: New Labour and the Return of Scotland, London: Granta Books.

Nicolson, S. (1999) 'New Plan Will Link Executive to Cabinet', The Scotsman November 29th.

Performance and Innovation Unit of the Cabinet Office (2000) Wiring It Up, London: The Stationery Office.

Royal Commission on the Reform of the House of Lords (chaired by Rt Hon Lord Wakeham) (2000) A House for the Future, London: The Stationery Office, Cm. 4534.

Rural Affairs Committee (1999a) 5th Report 1999: The Impact of the Scottish Adjacent Waters Boundaries Order, Edinburgh: The Stationery Office.

Rural Affairs Committee (1999b) 6th Report 1999: Interim Report on the

Agricultural Business Improvement Scheme, Edinburgh: The Stationery Office.

Sassoon, D. (1999) 'Convergence, Continuity and Change on the European Left', in G. Kelly (ed) The New European Left, London: Fabian Society, 7-19.

Schlesinger, P. (1998) 'Scottish Devolution and the Media', in J. Seaton (ed.) Politics and the Media: Harlots and Prerogatives at the Turn of the Millennium, Oxford: Blackwell Publishers, 55-74.

Scotland Act (1998), London: The Stationery Office.

Scott, D. (1999) 'Deacon Hits At MSPs' Claims She Was Evasive', The Scotsman, November 2nd.

Scottish Constitutional Convention (1995) Scotland's Parliament: Scotland's Right, Edinburgh: Convention of Scottish Local Authorities.

Scottish Executive (1999a) Fair Shares For All: Report of a Committee on Resources in the National Health Service in Scotland, Edinburgh: The Stationery Office.

Scottish Executive (1999b) Partnership for Scotland, Edinburgh: The Stationery Office.

Scottish Executive (1999c) Scottish Ministerial Code: A Code of Conduct and Guidance on Procedures for Members of the Scottish Executive and Junior Scottish Ministers, Edinburgh: The Stationery Office.

Scottish Executive (2000) Appointments to Public Bodies: Modernising the System, Consultation Paper, Edinburgh: The Stationery Office.

Scottish Law Commission (1991) 'Property Law: Abolition of the Feudal System', DP No. 93.

Scottish Law Commission (1999) 'Report on Abolition of the Feudal System', Scot Law Com 168.

Scottish Office (1997) Scotland's Parliament, Cm 3658, Edinburgh: The Scottish Office.

Scottish Parliament (1999) Official Report of the Scottish Parliament: June 16th, Edinburgh: The Stationery Office.

Sinclair, K. (2000) 'Smith turns fire against redneck rants', The Herald, May 20th.

Smith, M. (1994) Paper Lions: The Scottish Press and National Identity, Edinburgh: Polygon.

Surridge, P. and McCrone, D. (1999) 'The 1997 Scottish Referendum Vote', in B. Taylor and K. Thomson (eds) Scotland and Wales: Nations Again?, Cardiff: University of Wales Press, 41-64.

Taylor, R. (2000) 'Part time rules extended to agency staff', Financial Times, May 4th.

Transport and Environment Committee (2000) 3rd Report 2000: Report on inquiry into the proposals to introduce new planning procedures for telecommunications developments, Edinburgh: The Stationery Office.

Whaley J. and others (2000) Petitioners, First Division, Inner House of Court of Session, February 16th.

Wilson, R. (2000) Making a Difference: preparing the Programme for Government, Belfast: Democratic Dialogue.

# SUGGESTED READING

### General:

Christopher Harvie and Peter Jones, The Road to Home Rule: Images of Scotland's Cause, Edinburgh: Polygon 2000.
Murray Ritchie, Scotland Reclaimed: The Inside Story of Scotland's First Democratic Parliamentary Election, Edinburgh: The Saltire Society 2000.
Brian Taylor, The Scottish Parliament, Edinburgh: Polygon 1999.

### MSPs:

Michael Cavanagh, Neil McGarvey and Mark Shephard, New Scottish Parliament, New Scottish Parliamentarians?, Journal of Legislative Studies, forthcoming 2000.
Ann Packard, Instant Portraits: The Handbook of MSPs, Kircaldy: Ann Packard 1999.
Vacher's The Scottish Parliament, London: Vacher Dod Publishing 1999.

### Policies:

Gerry Hassan and Chris Warhurst (eds), A Different Future: A Modernisers' Guide to Scotland, Edinburgh: Centre for Scottish Public Policy/The Big Issue in Scotland 1999.
Eric Joyce (ed), Now's the Hour: New Thinking for Holyrood, London: Fabian Society 1999.
John McCarthy and David Newlands (eds), Governing Scotland: Problems and Prospects: The Economic Impact of the Scottish Parliament, Aldershot: Ashgate 1999.

### The 1997 General Election and Devolution Referendum:

Alice Brown, David McCrone, Lindsay Paterson and Paula Surridge, The Scottish Electorate: The 1997 General Election and Beyond, Basingstoke: Macmillan 1999.
David Denver, James Mitchell, Charles Pattie and Hugh Bochel, Scotland Decides: The Devolution Issue and the Scottish Referendum, London: Frank Cass 2000.
Bridget Taylor and Katarina Thomson (eds), Scotland and Wales: Nations Again?, Cardiff: University of Wales 1999.

**The 1999 Scottish Parliamentary Elections:**

David Denver, The Scottish Parliament Elections, *Politics Review*, Vol. 9 No. 1, September 1999, 30-33.
David Denver and Iain MacAllister, The Scottish Parliamentary Elections 1999: An Analysis of the Results, *Scottish Affairs*, no. 28. Summer 1999, 10-31.
Peter Jones, The 1999 Scottish Parliament Elections: From Anti-Tory to Anti-Nationalist Politics, *Scottish Affairs*, no. 28, Summer 1999, 1-9.

**British Dimensions:**

Vernon Bogdanor, Devolution in the United Kingdom, Oxford: Oxford University Press 1999.
Tom Nairn, After Britain: New Labour and the Return of Scotland, London: Granta Books 2000.

# INDEX

index

the new scottish politics the first year of the scottish parliament and beyond

Printed in the UK by The Stationery Office Limited 06/00 c17

**The Stationery Office publish a wide range of parliamentary publications to keep you up to date with developments in the Scottish Parliament.**

TSO is the official information provider and publisher for Parliament. Our data centre, based in the Scottish Parliament buildings, is responsible for the data management and publication of all parliamentary material, including Bills, Debates, Acts of Parliament plus Statutory Instruments and Command Papers.

To order any parliamentary publication, please contact our Scottish Customer Service Centre on **0870 606 5566**, order on line or visit our bookshop.

www.thestationeryoffice.com

The Stationery Office Bookshop
71 Lothian Road
Edinburgh
EH3 9AZ

code ALG

**The Stationery Office**

SCOTTISH
PARLIAMENTARY PUBLISHING

# TSO on behalf of the Scottish Parliament, publish a number of titles to keep you informed on developments and decisions made by Parliament.

**The Official Report - Plenary**
An authoritative report of parliamentary proceedings, detailing the day's debates and decisions made. Classification - 7001037.

**The Official Report - All Committees**
The report of all parliamentary committee proceedings. Classification - 66-25-011.

**Written Answers Report**
A weekly compilation of all written answers to Parliamentary Questions. Classification - 7002022.

**Business Bulletin**
A thorough parliamentary guide, including the day's business, forthcoming agendas and questions. Classification - 7001035.

**WHiSP - What's Happening in the Scottish Parliament**
A complete picture of parliamentary activities, detailing recent events and agendas for future business. - 7002021

The above publications are available to order on
Telephone Number - **0870 606 5566.**

code ALH